WO

GREATEST
COLLECTION
OF
CHURCH JOKES

THE
WORLD'S
GREATEST
COLLECTION
OF
CHURCH JOKES

NEARLY 500 HILARIOUS, GOOD-NATURED JOKES AND STORIES

Compiled and Edited by
Paul M. Miller

BARBOUR
PUBLISHING

Print ISBN 978-1-62416-701-0

eBook Editions:
Adobe Digital Edition (.epub) 978-1-60742-506-9
Kindle and MobiPocket Edition (.prc) 978-1-60742-507-6

Published by Barbour Publishing, Inc., P.O. Box 719, Uhrichsville, Ohio 44683, www.barbourbooks.com

Our mission is to publish and distribute inspirational products offering exceptional value and biblical encouragement to the masses.

Member of the
Evangelical Christian
Publishers Association

Printed in the United States of America.

CONTENTS

RX FOR FUNNY BONES

"A cheerful heart is good medicine"
(Proverbs 17:22 NIV).

Back when our feet didn't touch the sanctuary floor (in a pew, that is), we knew that the church was nothing to laugh at. But, admit it, then and today, there are those times when pew-to-pew solemnity can't prevent our funny bones from kicking in— even with near-blood-producing lip biting and horrific visions of family tragedy.

What this oversize collection of old, new, and not so true church rib-ticklers has going for it, is the recognition that whether we worship in high church fashion, easygoing informality, or any place in between, we have at least one thing in common—we like to laugh. Contrary to our parents' opinion, the devil doesn't make us do it. The good Lord implanted the funny bone as surely as He did our souls. Let's enjoy it!

Give me a sense of humor, Lord,
Give me the grace to see a joke,
To get some humor out of life
And pass it on to other folk.

AUTHOR UNKNOWN

PASTORS

You'll not find any of those "There was a priest, a minister, and a rabbi" jokes in this section—there are just too many of them; golf gags have been limited to two.

The clergy has always and will always be a target for good-natured ribbing. Their fabled foibles, like sleep-producing preaching and only Sunday work will always be good-natured jabs for the pew-sitters to level. It's all good fun. Pass on some of these golden oldies to your spiritual leader. Laugh together and strike a bargain, though, that you never become a sermon illustration.

Anyway, as Mark Twain's non sequitur goes, "Sacred cows make the best hamburger."

A PENNY SAVED. . .

Hoping to help his church save money, Pastor Jones decided to paint the church exterior himself, but all he had on hand was one bucket of paint. So he collected a bunch of empty buckets and some water, which he used to thin the paint enough to cover the building. Then he spent the whole day painting.

That night it rained and washed off all the paint. The pastor was so discouraged and asked God, "Why. . .why Lord, did you let it rain and wash away all my hard work?" To which God replied, "Repaint and thin no more!"

AND NOTHING BUT THE TRUTH

Friend: Say, Pastor, how is it that you're so thin and gaunt while your horse is so fat and sleek?

Pastor: Because I feed the horse and the congregation feeds me.

A Golf Joke

Pastor Teefer found himself wondering whether there were any golf courses in heaven. He even began to ask the question in his prayers. One day, in answer to his prayers, he received a direct answer from on high.

"Yes," said the heavenly messenger, "there are many excellent golf courses in heaven. The greens are always in first-class condition, the weather is always perfect, and you always play with the nicest people."

"Oh, thank you," responded Preacher Teefer. "That really is marvelous news."

"Yes, isn't it?" replied the messenger. "And we've got you down for a foursome next Saturday."

One More

A clergyman took a well-earned holiday and decided to go to one of those large golf resorts where Arnold Palmer often played.

As the minister approached the most

difficult hole on the course, the caddie said, "When Arnold Palmer plays this hole, he uses a three-iron and says a prayer."

"I'll certainly give it a try," the preacher remarked. But when the ball landed in the water, he said, "I guess the Lord didn't hear me."

"He probably heard you," the caddie said, "but when Arnold Palmer says his prayers, he keeps his head down."

BIG FISHERMAN

A very upset minister walked into the fish market. "I want you to throw me four big fish," he said to the clerk. "Just toss 'em to me."

"But why toss them to you?" the fish-monger asked. "Can't I just wrap them and give them to you like everyone else?"

"No, sir!" yelled the preacher. "Do just as I say. So if anyone asks me if I caught any fish today, I can truthfully say, 'Sure did. Caught four big ones!'"

PRAYER FOR SAFETY

A nearsighted minister glanced at the note that Mrs. Jones had sent to him by an usher. The note read, "Bill Jones having gone to sea, his wife desires the prayers of the congregation for his safety."

Failing to note the punctuation, the cleric startled his audience by announcing, "Bill Jones, having gone to see his wife, desires the prayers of the congregation for his safety."

SPELLING ONE

Board Chair: Pastor, why did you fire your secretary?

Pastor: She couldn't spell. She kept asking me how to spell about every other word while she took dictation.

Board Chair: I suppose you couldn't stand the interruptions.

Pastor: No, it wasn't that. I just didn't have time to look up all those words.

SPELLING TWO

Pastor: I need a secretary who can spell. Can you spell Mississippi?

Hopeful Secretary: The river or the state?

MOWER AND MOWER

Pastor Sampson was making visitation rounds on his trusty bicycle, when he turned a corner and came upon a young boy trying to sell a lawn mower. "How much do you want for it?" Sampson asked.

"I just need enough money to buy a bicycle," the boy explained. After a moment of thought, the preacher asked, "Will you take my bike in trade for it?"

"Mister, you've got yourself a deal."

The preacher took the mower and began to crank it. He pulled on the cord a few times with no reaction from the machine. The preacher called the boy over and said, "I can't get this mower to start."

The little boy said, "My dad says you

have to cuss at it to get it started."

Pastor Sampson replied, "I am a minister, and I cannot cuss. I have been saved for so long I don't even remember how to cuss."

The little boy look at him with a sparkle in his eye, "Just keep pulling on that cord, and it'll come back to you."

NEW PASTOR WARRANTY

It has come to our attention that the pastor you received was shipped with a slight defect—he is not psychic. Because of this, you must observe certain procedures to ensure optimum performance.

It is necessary to inform him of any members who are hospitalized.

If someone you know is in need of prayer, the pastor must be told, or he won't know.

If you are in need of a pastoral visit, you will get best results if you ask him.

We regret any inconvenience this may cause.

SUNDAY MORNING

A mother called her son on Sunday morning to make sure he got out of bed and was ready for church.

"I'm not going," he replied.

"Yes, you are going, so get out of that bed!" his mother demanded.

"Give me one good reason why I should go," said her son.

"I'll give you three good reasons. One, I'm your mother, and I say you're going. Two, you're forty years old, so you're old enough to know better. And three, you're the pastor, so you need to be there."

DECAF OR REGULAR?

Every Sunday morning at the same point in the service, Pastor Fred left the platform for a brief time to talk to the kids in children's church. One new member didn't understand what was going on, so following the service he observed, "Preacher, you are the first pastor I ever saw who takes a coffee break during the service."

MAIL CALL

The postman had just delivered Reverend Smith's mail. As the cleric opened envelopes and pulled out letters, he was surprised to unfold a sheet of paper that bore just one word, "Fool." The next Sunday he announced, "I have known many people who have written letters and forgot to sign their names. But this week I received a letter from someone who signed his name, but forgot to write a letter."

PASTORAL PERFECTION

Good news! After hundreds of years of ministers, a model pastor has been found—one who will please every church member.

He is twenty-six years old and has been preaching for thirty years. He is tall, short, thin, heavyset, handsome, and has one brown eye and one blue eye. His hair is parted in the middle (blonde), left side (dark and straight), and on the right side (brown and wavy).

He has a burning desire to work with teenagers and spends all his time with older folks. He smiles all the time with a straight face because he has a sense of humor that keeps him seriously dedicated to his work.

He makes fifteen calls a day on church members, spends all his time evangelizing the lost, and never leaves his office.

A Grave Error

A minister on vacation was reading his hometown newspaper. He was stunned to come across his own obituary. Shocked, and not a little upset, he immediately telephoned the editor.

"I'm calling you long distance about the report of my death in your paper yesterday," he explained with great indignation.

"Yes, sir," came the calm reply. "And from where are you calling?"

PRISON BLUES

The preacher was visiting a man in prison. "When you were tempted," asked the minister, "why didn't you say, 'Get thee behind me, Satan!'?"

"I did," replied the prisoner, "but Satan said, 'It doesn't matter who leads, since we're both going the same direction.'"

HALT!

When a traffic cop pulled over Pastor Johnson for speeding, the minister reminded the officer, "Blessed are the merciful, for they shall obtain mercy." The cop handed the minister the ticket and quoted, "Go thou and sin no more."

SLEEPERS

Reverend Nick: I worry so much, I can't sleep at night and have terrible nightmares.

Reverend Rick: That's nothing. I'm sleeping like a baby. I wake up every three hours and cry.

UNREPEATABLE STORIES

Delivering a building fund-raising banquet speech on the night of his arrival in a large city, a visiting minister told several anecdotes that he expected to repeat at meetings the next day. Because he wanted to tell the jokes over again, he requested the reporters to omit them from any accounts they might submit to their newspapers.

A cub reporter, in commenting on the speech, ended his piece with these words: "The minister told a number of stories that cannot be printed."

TRUTH OR CARE

One Sunday morning Pastor Bob advised his congregation, "Next week I plan to preach about the sin of lying. In preparation for my message. I want you all to read Mark 17."

The following Sunday the reverend asked for a show of hands from those who had read Mark 17. Every hand went up. Pastor Bob smiled and announced, "Well, Mark has only sixteen chapters. I will now proceed with my sermon on the sin of lying."

WHOOPS!

My Protestant clergy friend was speaking with a Catholic priest and wanted to establish a solid friendship. He spoke of many things and felt it was going well, but in an instant he undid all the good he'd done: He asked if Father Paddy's father had been a priest, too.

A Confession

The Reverend Billy Graham tells of a time early in his ministry when he arrived in a small town to preach a revival meeting. Wanting to mail a letter, he asked a young boy where the post office was. When the boy had told him, Dr. Graham thanked him and said, "If you'll come to the church this evening, you can hear me give directions on how to get to heaven."

"I don't think I'll be there," the boy replied. "You don't even know how to get to the post office."

Politically Speaking

The minister of Grace Church phoned the city's newspaper. "Thank you very much," he said, "for the error you made when you printed my sermon title on the church page. The topic I sent you was 'What Jesus Saw in a Publican.' You printed it as 'What Jesus Saw in a Republican.' I had the largest crowd of the year."

You're a Preacher If. . .

The most popular feature in a recent denominational clergy magazine is titled "You Might Be a Preacher If. . ." Here are a few unsolicited examples of ways readers completed that sentence:

"You've been told to get a real job."

"You've been tempted to name your fishing boat 'Visitation.' "

"You couldn't sell used cars."

"You never said, 'I'm NEVER going to be a preacher!' "

"You win a door prize at the church banquet, and people say it was rigged."

"Your belly is ever referred to as 'the chicken coop.' "

"Your kids nickname you 'Our father who art at a meeting.' "

Same for Missionaries and Their Kids

"You don't think two hours is a long sermon."

"You refer to gravel roads as highways."

"Fitting fifteen or more people into a car seems normal."

"You realize that furlough is not a vacation."

"You do your devotions in another language."

"You speak with authority on the subject of airline travel."

"You can cut grass with a machete but can't start a lawnmower."

"You watch nature documentaries and think how good that animal would taste if it were fried."

"You can't answer the question, 'Where are you from?'"

WALKING OUT

"I hope you didn't take it personally, Reverend," an embarrassed woman said after church service, "when my husband walked out during your sermon."

"I did find it rather disconcerting," the preacher replied.

"It's not a reflection on you, sir," insisted the churchgoer. "Ralph has been walking in his sleep ever since he was a child."

BOWLING

Did you hear the one about the ministers who formed a bowling team? Called themselves the Holy Rollers.

BARE ESSENTIALS

When the new First Church pastor came to town, one of his first official activities was to visit his parishioners. All went well until he knocked on the Jones's door. It was obvious that someone was home, but no one came to the door.

Finally he took out his card and wrote on the back, "Revelation 3:20, 'Behold, I stand at the door and knock: if any man hear my voice, and open the door, I will come in to him,'" and stuck it in the door.

On Sunday his card found its way into

the offering plate. Below his message was the notation, "Genesis 3:10, 'And he said, I heard thy voice in the garden, and I was afraid, because I was naked; and I hid myself.' "

AT THE CEMETERY

A newly appointed young minister was contacted by the local funeral director to hold a graveside service in a small country cemetery. Because the deceased had no friends or family left, there was to be no funeral, just the committal.

The pastor started to the cemetery early enough, but he soon lost his way, causing him to arrive thirty minutes late. There was no hearse or funeral director in sight, just the workmen, who were sitting under a tree eating lunch. Moving to the newly dug grave, the minister opened his prayer book and read the service over the vault lid that was in place.

When returning to his car, the preacher overheard one of the workman say, "Maybe we'd better tell him that's a septic tank."

WHOSE WAY?

Said the revival preacher to the stately old Presbyterian cleric: "After all, we are both doing the Lord's work—you in your way, and I in His."

SERMON AID

The reverend got up and strode to his pulpit with a patch on his chin: "I'm sorry about the bandage, but I cut my chin shaving thinking about my sermon." A voice from the congregation called out, "Next time, why not think about your chin and cut the sermon?"

FARMERS KNOW

On a very cold, snowy Sunday in February, only the minister and one farmer arrived at the village church. The minister observed, "Well, I don't guess we'll have a service today." To which the farmer replied, "If only one cow shows up at feeding time, I feed it."

Remember This One?

The new preacher at Dry Gulch Community Church was so nervous about delivering his first sermon that he'd not gotten much sleep for several nights. Matter of fact, he was so tired he could barely make it up the steps to his pulpit. Fortunately, he found his text and began preaching. But nervousness soon overtook him, and the outline flew right out of his mind.

Now, in Bible school he'd been taught that if a lapse of memory occurs, it is wise to repeat your last point. And so he did. "Behold," he quoted, "I come quickly," but his mind was still a blank. He tried one more time, still no memory of what was to come next. Another attempt, but no results.

Finally he stepped way back, made a lunge toward the pulpit, shouted out, "Behold, I come quickly," tripped, and fell into the lap of a little old lady in the front row. Flustered and embarrassed, he picked himself up, apologized profusely, and started to explain what had happened. "That's all right, young man," said the kindly old lady. "It was really my fault. You warned me three times that you were on your way down here. I should have just gotten out of your way."

PEW-SITTERS

Hey, don't get in an uproar. This is not a put-down of church laity—it means exactly what it says. These are jokes about us who sit in the pews, as opposed to those who sit up by the pulpit. Pew-sitting is an honorable profession. If it weren't for us, the pulpit sitters would have no one to preach to. And remember, some thinker somewhere said this: "A good sense of humor helps us pew-sitters in many ways. It helps us understand the orthodox, tolerate the unpleasant, overcome the unexpected, and survive the unbearable."

AN EVALUATION

Clara: My pastor is so good he can preach on any subject for an hour.

Sarah: That's nothing! My pastor can talk for an hour without a subject.

FAST READERS

The parson had been disturbed by a person who read much too fast during responsive readings.

"We shall now read the Twenty-third Psalm—in unison." He paused. "Will the lady who is always 'by still waters' while the rest of us are 'in green pastures,' please wait a minute until we catch up?"

BEDSIDE MANNER

A lonesome woman parishioner demanded a home visit from her pastor. So, as promised, the reverend showed up and sat by the woman's bed listening to her litany of woe. Finally he asked to read some passages from her Bible.

In a much-too-sweet voice she called to her little daughter playing in the next room, "Darling, please bring Mother that dear old book that she reads every night." Promptly the little girl brought in a copy of a popular TV-movie magazine.

THE TATE FAMILY MEMBERS

Do you have any idea of how many members of the Tate family belong to your congregation? There is old man Dic Tate who wants to run everything, while uncle Ro Tate tries to change everything. Their sister, Agi Tate, stirs up plenty of trouble with help from her husband, Irri Tate. Whenever new projects are suggested, Hesi Tate and his wife Vegi Tate want to wait until next year. Brother Facili Tate is quite helpful in church business. Cousins Cogi Tate and Medi Tate always think things over and lend a helpful steady hand. And, of course, there is the bad seed in the family, Ampu Tate, who has cut himself off completely from the Body of Christ.

LAITY THOUGHTS

There are four classes of church members: the tired, the retired, the tiresome, and the tireless.

Every church has three classes of members: the workers, the jerkers, and the shirkers.

Some church members who say "Our Father" on Sunday go around the rest of the week acting like orphans.

It seems that some church members have been starched and ironed, but too few have been washed.

DICTIONARY OF CHURCH ATTENDERS:

Pillars—worship regularly, giving time and money; Leaners—use the church for funerals, baptisms, and weddings; Specials—help and give occasionally for something that appeals to them; Annuals—dress up for Easter and come for Christmas programs; Sponges—take all blessing and benefits, even the sacraments, but never give out anything themselves; Scrappers—take offense and criticize.

A Confession

The chief trouble with the church is that you and I are in it.

Caught in the Acts

Sister Deena had just returned home from Sunday evening service when she was startled by a burglar. With great biblical authority she yelled, "Stop! Acts 2:38!", which implies "Turn from your sin."

The thief stopped dead in his tracks. Then the woman calmly called the police and explained what she had done.

As the officer cuffed the man, he asked the burglar, "Why did you stop your burgling? All the old lady did was yell a Bible verse at you."

"Bible verse?" replied the crook. "She said she had an ax and two .38s!"

PEW-SITTERS COME FORWARD

According to a not-so-scientific-study, here are the top ten reasons to sit at the front of the church:

1. Statistics show that the front of the church building is the safest in the event of a natural disaster.
2. You can easily see who comes forward to pray during the invitation.
3. There's still lots of padding in these seats since they're almost like new.
4. You only have to comb the back of your hair and iron the back of your shirt.
5. It's easier not to be seen passing the offering plate by.
6. No one will hear your stomach make all those "alien" noises as noon nears.
7. You can keep a practiced eye on changes in choir members' hair color and styles.
8. You want to justify the feeling you've always had that everyone's looking at you.

9. It's an ideal place to keep from seeing how your teens behave during
   the service.
10. You actually love worshiping God
    and feeding on His Word!

THEN THERE WAS SISTER ANNIE

Last Sunday, Annie's pastor challenged
his congregation to be aware of opportu-
nities to testify for Jesus. Now Annie was
certainly known for her faith and her
boldness in talking about the Lord. She
was known to stand on her front porch
and for the benefit of her atheist neighbor, shout, "Praise the Lord!" resulting in
her godless neighbor's response, "There
ain't no God!"

When hard times set in, Annie stood
on her porch and prayed, "Praise the Lord!
Please God, send me some groceries." The
next morning she found a large bag of groceries on her porch, which caused her to
shout, "Praise the Lord!"

On cue, her neighbor jumped out from

behind a bush and cried, "Hey, don't give God the credit—I bought those groceries, He didn't!"

Annie laughed, jumped up and down, clapped her hands, and shouted, "Praise the Lord! He not only sent me groceries, but he made the devil pay for them!"

LAY ADVICE

A successful layman was in a great deal of business trouble.

In no uncertain terms the enterprise was failing. Even though he put in every penny he and the bank had, he owed everybody. It was so bad, he contemplated suicide. As a last resort he went to a pastor and with many tears asked for help.

When the businessman finished his story, his pastor said, "Here's what I want you to do: Take a beach chair and your Bible and head down to the beach. When you get there, take the beach chair and your Bible and sit at the water's edge.

Next, you shall open your Bible; the wind will riffle the pages, but finally the breeze will die down. Look down at the page and read the first thing you see. From that you will know what to do."

A year later the businessman went back to the pastor and brought his wife and children with him. The man was in a new custom-tailored suit, his wife wore a mink coat, and the children looked like fashion plates. The businessman pulled out an envelope stuffed with money and gave it to the pastor as a thank-you gift.

The pastor recognized the businessman and was curious. "You did as I suggested?" he asked.

"Absolutely," replied the businessman.

"You went to the beach?"

"Absolutely."

"You sat in the beach chair with the Bible in your lap?"

"Absolutely."

"You let the pages riffle until they stopped?"

"Absolutely."

"And what were the first words you saw on the page?"

"Chapter 11."

SHIPWRECKED CHURCHMAN

One balmy evening in the South Pacific, a navy ship spied smoke coming from one of three huts on an uncharted island.

Upon arriving at the shore, the crew was met by a shipwreck survivor. He said, "I'm so glad you're here. I've been alone on this island for more than five years."

The captain replied, "If you're all alone, why do I see three huts?"

The survivor answered, "Well, I live in one and go to church in another."

"What about the third hut?" asked the captain.

"That's where I used to go to church."

TRANSPARENT COMPLIMENT

The pastor of St. Paul's Church was ill one

Sunday morning, so a preacher was called as pulpit supply. In his opening remarks the preacher said, "You know, a substitute preacher is like a piece of cardboard in a broken window. He fills the space, but after all, he's not the real glass."

After the service, a lady approached the preacher trying to pay him a compliment. "You weren't a replacement after all. You were a real pane."

CONVERSATION

Coming out of church, Mrs. Peterson asks her husband, "Do you think that Johnson girl is putting a rinse on her hair?"

"I didn't even see her," Mr. Peterson admits.

"And the dress Martha Hansen was wearing," Mrs. Peterson continues, "really, don't tell me you think that's the proper outfit for a mother of two."

"I'm afraid I didn't notice that, either," Mr. Peterson says.

"Oh, for heaven's sake," Mrs. Peterson snaps, "a lot of good it does for you to go to church."

OUR CHURCH WILL BE PERFECT WHEN WE HEAR. . .

1. "Hey! It's my turn to sit in the front pew."
2. "I was so enthralled, I never noticed your sermon went twenty-five minutes overtime."
3. "Personally, I find witnessing much more enjoyable than golf."
4. "I dearly want to be a teacher in the junior high Sunday school class."
5. "Forget the denominational minimum salary; let's pay our pastor so he can live like we do."
6. "I love it when we sing hymns I've never heard before."
7. "Since we're all here, let's start the service early."

8. "Nothing inspires me and strengthens my commitment like our annual stewardship campaign."
9. "Pastor, we'd like to send you to this continuing education seminar in the Bahamas."
10. "I've decided to give our church the five hundred dollars a month I used to send to TV evangelists."

A Little off the Sides

Right in the middle of his sermon, verbose Pastor Phillips noted Brother Bob get up and leave the sanctuary; then he returned before the closing hymn.

Afterwards Pastor Phillips asked, "Where did you go, Brother Bob?"

"I went to get a haircut," was Bob's reply.

"But why didn't you do that before the service?" asked the reverend.

"Because I didn't need one then."

TURN OFF THE GAS

Right in the middle of the service and just before the sermon, a soprano in the choir remembered she had forgotten to turn down the heat under the Sunday roast. Hurriedly she scribbled a note and passed it to the usher to give to her husband.

Unfortunately, the usher misunderstood and took it to the pulpit. Unfolding the note, the preacher read, "Please go home and turn off the gas."

APPROPRIATE DRESS

The rural Baptist church had a small congregation of mostly very faithful people. "Mostly" because one brother, Ethan Jones, had quit coming to church. The pastor became concerned about Jones, so he went out to his farm and asked why he didn't come anymore.

"Well, Preacher, I only have these overalls and old boots. I can't go to the Lord's house dressed like this."

"I can remedy that," declared the pastor. "I've got a spare shirt, sports coat, slacks, and shoes that I'll give to you if you'll come back to church."

The man agreed, and the pastor came back that afternoon with the clothes.

Next Sunday Ethan Jones didn't show up again. So the pastor went out to the farm and asked, "I gave you all those clothes; why didn't you come to church?"

"Well, Preacher," Jones responded, "I got up and showered and shaved, and I put on those neat duds, and I looked in the mirror. I looked so good that I went to the Episcopal church in town."

SUNDAY STUPOR

Miss Gladys was a regular fixture in morning worship at First Church. On this one particular morning the pastor's message went on forever. Some in the congregation dozed off.

Following the service, she walked up to

a very sleepy looking visitor to welcome him. "Hello, I'm Gladys Dunn."

To which the visitor replied, "You're not the only one."

SILENT WITNESS

A rural church attender found himself in New York City on the Lord's Day. Right across the street from his hotel was a huge gothic church with the tallest steeple he had ever seen. He decided to attend service there. Entering the sanctuary he found an atmosphere far different from his country church back home. The pipe organ and formally dressed ushers seemed strange, but they didn't deter him from shouting out "Amen" when the minister made a particularly good point. Everyone in the church turned around and stared, and an usher came running down the aisle.

"You must not talk out loud," warned the usher.

"But," protested the rustic visitor, "I've got religion."

"Well," said the usher, "you did not get it here."

HEALTHY CHRISTIANS

Bert and Ernie are two Christians who have lived very good and healthy lives. They die and arrive in heaven. Walking along one of the golden streets and marveling at all the paradise around them, Ernie turns to Bert and says, "Wow. I never knew heaven was going to be as good as this."

"Yeah," says Bert. "And just think, if we hadn't eaten all that oat bran, we could have gotten here ten years earlier."

PRAY-ERS

Folks who pray are certainly in the majority around here. That's always a good sign. What's really interesting is that most of the quips about prayer focus on kids. Funny thing, most of them have kids saying exactly what some of us have thought at one time or another. Like this:

Mother: "That's no way to say your prayers, honey."

Honey: "But, Mom, I thought that God was tired of hearing the same old stuff every night. So I told him the story of the Three Bears instead."

Makes you kind of think, hmm?

ELECTRONIC PRAYERS

A mother was teaching her three-year-old daughter the Lord's Prayer. For several evenings at bedtime, she repeated it after her mother. One night she said she was ready to try it on her own. Mother glowed with pride and listened to each word right up to the end. "And lead us not into temptation," she prayed, "but deliver us some E-mail. Amen."

DESPERATE PRAYING

Worshipers at All Saints Church were invited to a special Lenten study on prayer. At the close of the course Pastor Nixon invited the participants to write sentence prayers. Here are some of those prayers.

"Lord, help me to relax about insignificant details—beginning at 7:41:23 A.M., EST."

"God, help me to consider people's feelings, even if most of them are hypersensitive."

"Father, help me take responsibility for my own actions, even though they're usually not my fault."

"Dear God, help me not try to run everything. But if you need some help, feel free to ask me."

"Lord, help me to be more laid back, and help me do it exactly right."

"Heavenly Father, please help me take things more seriously, especially having a good time."

"God, give me patience, and I mean right now!"

"Lord, help me not to be a perfectionist. (Did I spell that correctly?)"

"Lord, keep me open to other people's ideas, wrong though they may be."

"Dear God, help me to slowdownandnotrushthroughwhatIdo."

Amen.

HONEST PRAYING

Minister: "So your mother says your prayers with you every night? What does she say?"

Little Boy: "Thank God, he's in bed."

PRAYER WARRIOR

A deeply religious man was perched on his roof loudly praying while floodwaters licked at his feet. His pastor came by in a boat and said, "Get in!" The religious man replied, "No, I'm up here praying, and I know God will grant me a miracle."

Later the water was up to his waist, and another boat floated by and that rescuer yelled for him to get in. The pray-er responded that God would answer his prayers and give him a miracle.

With the water chin high, a helicopter threw down a rope ladder and told him to climb to safety. He again turned down the offer. "My prayers will be answered."

Finally he gulped his last breath and found himself at the gates of heaven. With broken faith he cried to St. Peter, "I thought God would grant me a miracle. He let me down."

"I don't know why you're complaining." St. Peter chuckled. "We sent you two boats and a helicopter."

BREAKFAST

Every evening, a mother and her young
son knelt down beside his bed so he could
say his prayers. One night, obviously bored
with the same old prayer, the little boy ear-
nestly prayed, "Now I lay me down to
sleep, I pray the Lord my soul to keep. If
I should die before I wake—can I have
breakfast with You in the morning?"

BULLETIN SQUIB

"If your troubles are deep-seated and long-
standing, then try kneeling."

GIVING THANKS

It was the church's annual Christmas
dinner, and little Ben was asked to return
thanks. The church members bowed their
heads, and Ben began his prayer, thanking God for all his friends, naming them
one by one. Then he thanked God for

Mommy, Daddy, brother, sister, Grandma, Grandpa, all his aunts and uncles, Pastor Wright and Mrs. Wright, their kids, and his Sunday school class. Then he began thanking God for the food. He prayed a mighty thank-you for the turkey, the dressing, the fruit salads, the cranberry sauces, the pies, even the Cool Whip.

Then he paused, and everyone waited. After a long silence, the young boy looked up at his mother and asked, "If I thank God for Mrs. Wright's broccoli casserole, won't He know I'm lying?"

FROM A CHILD'S HEART

A daddy was listening to his child say her prayers. "Dear Harold. . ."

"Wait a minute, honey, how come you called God 'Harold'?"

The little girl looked up and said, "That's what they call Him in church. You know the prayer we say, 'Our Father, who art in heaven, Harold be Thy name.'"

And then there was this particular four-year-old who prayed, "And forgive us our trash baskets as we forgive those who put trash in our baskets."

And finally, the realist: "Dear God, please take care of my daddy and my mommy and my sister and my brother and my doggy and me. Oh, yes, please take care of yourself, God. If anything happens to You, we're gonna be in a big mess."

A Scot's Offering Prayer

In Scotland there have been times when collection plates were rarely full. During one of those dry periods, an old Presbyterian cleric looked down at the returned receptacle plate and prayed, "Well, Lord, we thank you for the safe return of the plate."

TV Prayer

"Lord, comfort those who are afflicted by their TV sets today."

WHISTLE WHILE YOU PRAY

During the minister's prayer one Sunday, there was a loud whistle from one of the back pews. Gary's mother was horrified. She pinched him into silence and after church asked, "Gary, whatever made you do such a thing?"

Gary answered soberly, "I asked God to teach me to whistle—and He just then did!"

PRAYER FOR THE DEAF

It was bedtime for Timmy and Jimmy who were staying overnight with their grandparents. While kneeling to say his prayers, Timmy began praying at the top of his lungs, "Dear God, for Christmas I want some video games, a motor bike, a DVD player. . ."

"Whoa," Jimmy hollered, "Why are you yelling? God ain't deaf."

"I know God's not deaf," replied Timmy. "But Grandma is!"

AMEN

During a children's sermon, Reverend Larry asked the boys and girls what the word "amen" means. Little Chucky's hand shot up, "I know," he chirped. "It means, 'Tha-tha-tha-that's all folks!'"

HELPFUL PRAYER

Timmy had been misbehaving in children's church and was isolated from the other children for time-out. After awhile he emerged and informed his teacher that he had thought it over and then prayed about it.

"Fine," said his pleased teacher. "If you ask God to help you not to misbehave, He will help you."

"Oh, I didn't ask Him that," said Timmy, "I asked Him to help you put up with me."

HERE GOES. . .

"So far today, God, I've done all right. I haven't gossiped, haven't lost my temper, haven't been selfish, grumpy, nasty, or overindulgent. I'm really glad about that.

"But in a few minutes, God, I'm going to get out of bed, and from then on I'm probably going to need a lot more help.

"Thank you. In Jesus' name, amen."

A QUICK GRACE

The pastor was invited over for dinner and asked to lead in prayer for the meal. After a brief prayer, Little Fred said approvingly, "You don't pray so long when you're hungry, do you?"

LAUGHTER

A small girl was reprimanded by her mother for giggling during prayer. "It's okay, Mom," she explained. "I was just sharing a joke with God."

Dennis began to fall out a tree and cried out, "Lord, save me, save me!" There was a pause, and then he said, "Never mind, Lord, my pants just got caught on a branch."

DEAR PASTOR. . .

"Please pray for all the airplane pilots. I am flying to California tomorrow." Laurie, age ten.

TRUISM

After attending a prayer meeting where everyone prayed very loudly, a little kid remarked, "If they lived nearer to God, they wouldn't have to pray so loud."

NOT TO WORRY

Seven-year-old Mark was overheard praying, "Lord, if you can't make me a better boy, don't worry about it. I'm having a real good time like I am."

A Matter of Perspective

Three clergymen were deep in a discussion of the best positions for praying while a telephone repairman worked nearby.

"Kneeling is definitely best," claimed one.

"No," another contended. "I get the best results standing with my arms outstretched to heaven."

"You're both wrong," the third argued. "The most effective prayer position is lying on the floor facedown."

The telephone repairman could contain himself no longer. "Hey, guys," he interrupted, "the best prayin' I ever did was hangin' upside down from a telephone pole."

"Thanks a Lot, Lord"

Little Anna's father drove the family home from church. After washing their hands Anna and her father sat at the table. Anna's mother brought heaping plates of dinner and set them in front of the girl and her daddy. As he always did,

Anna's father grumbled about the meal, then asked the blessing.

Looking confused, Little Anna asked, "Daddy, does God hear us when we pray?"

"Why, of course, Anna," he replied. "He hears us every time we pray."

"And does He hear everything we say the rest of the time?"

"Yes, every word," he answered, encouraged that he had inspired his daughter to be curious about spiritual matters.

Innocently she burst his bubble with her next question. "Then which does God believe?"

CHOW DOWN

The minister's son was invited to his friend's house for dinner. Before they ate, the boy bowed his head and waited for the blessing to be said. But everyone else started helping themselves to the food, and he looked up puzzled.

"What's wrong? Why aren't you eating?" asked his friend's mom.

The boy, who had been taught to give thanks, asked, "Don't you pray at meals?"

The father answered they didn't.

"Oh, I see," said the boy, "you're just like my dog—you start right in."

NEXT TO NOTHING

A local church pastor, burdened by the importance of his work, went into the sanctuary to pray. Falling to his knees, he lamented, "O Lord, I am nothing! I am nothing."

The minister of education passed by, and overhearing the prayer, was moved to join the pastor on his knees. Shortly he, too, was crying aloud, "O Lord, I too am nothing. I am nothing."

The janitor of the church, awed by the sight of the two men praying, joined them crying, "O Lord, I also am nothing. I am nothing."

At this, the minister of education nudged his senior pastor and said, "Now look who thinks he's nothing."

THE CHURCH OFFICE
AND STAFF

Dozens of people have expressed the opinion that church secretaries have been completely overlooked in receiving recognition for their devotion to pastor and staff, and for laboring above and beyond what they thought they were getting themselves into when they took the job.

The dozens mentioned above say that church secretaries should have their own version of the Purple Heart. Others have suggested induction into the Ecclesiastical Order of Jammed Photocopiers, a worldwide sisterhood for those who have fearlessly stuck newly manicured fingers into the inner workings of the office behemoth. Male secretaries will have to find their own recognition.

Nothing but great admiration will you find on these pages for the keepers of parish records and secrets.

JOB EVALUATION

Pastor: "I was just reading over this letter you did. Your typing is really improving. I see there are only seven mistakes here."

Secretary: "Thank you, Brother Smith."

Pastor: "Now, let's take a look at the second line."

THE ELECTRONIC SECRETARY

As church secretary you may be obsessing over your computer when. . .

You turn off your computer and get an awful empty feeling, as if you just pulled the plug on a loved one.

You start using smileys :-) in your snail mail.

You find yourself typing "com" after every period when using a word processor. com

You can't correspond with your mother, since she doesn't have a computer.

In real life conversations, you don't laugh, you just say, "LOL, LOL."

You move into a new house and you decide to "Netscape" before you landscape.

When your inbox shows "no new messages," you feel really depressed.

You wake up at four o'clock in the morning to go to the bathroom and stop to check your E-mail on the way back to bed.

You don't know the gender of your three closest friends because they have nondescript screen names and you never bothered to ask.

DONATIONS ACCEPTED

When church secretary Ms. Daisy answered the ringing phone, a man's voice asked, "Can I speak to the head hog at the trough?" The secretary thought she heard what he said, but asked, "I'm sorry, who?" The caller repeated, "Can I speak to the head hog at the trough?"

Daisy thought a moment and then answered, "If you mean the preacher, then you may refer to him as 'Pastor,' or 'Brother,' but I'd prefer that you not refer to him as the 'head hog at the trough'!"

To this, the man replied, "Well, I was wanting to give one hundred thousand dollars to the building fund."

Quick as a wink, Daisy responded, "Hang on, sir, I believe I just heard his 'oink.' "

Confession

Secretary: "I type by the biblical system."
Deacon: "What is that?"
Secretary: "The 'seek and ye shall find' system."

From the Office Bulletin Board

Did you hear the one about the office worker who ran out of sick days, so he called in dead?

I hate housework. You make the beds, you do the dishes—and six months later you have to start all over again.

Tarzan came home from a hard day's work and said, "Jane, it's a jungle out there."

A Nasty Letter

After receiving a mean-spirited letter from one of his members, Pastor Bob went into the church office and dictated the following to his secretary:

"The enclosed letter arrived on my desk a few days ago. I am sending it to you because I think you ought to know that some idiot is sending out letters over your signature. Cordially. . ."

Tardy

Every day Reverend's secretary was twenty minutes late. Then one day she slid snugly in place only five minutes late.

"Well," said her boss, "this is the earliest you've ever been late."

EXPERIENCE PAYS

Reverend: "In this church secretary job we need someone who is responsible."

Applicant: "That's me! In my last job, when anything went wrong, they said I was responsible."

THOSE BULLETIN GOOFS

These have been the bane of every church secretary. No one can vouch for their authenticity, but they're fair warning for the church staff.

"Thursday night—Potluck supper. Prayer and medication to follow."

"For those of you who have children and don't know it, we have a nursery downstairs."

"This being Easter Sunday, Mrs. Bertha Lewis will come forward and lay an egg on the altar."

"Next Sunday a special collection
will be taken to defray the cost
of the new carpeting.
All those wishing to do something
on the new carpet will come
forward and do it."

"During the absence of our pastor,
we enjoyed the rare privilege of hearing
a good sermon when Dr. A. B. Doe
supplied our pulpit."

"You will want to attend
the National Prayer and Fasting
Conference at First Church.
Your registration fee includes three meals."

"Ladies, don't forget the rummage sale.
It's a chance to get rid of those things
you don't want to keep.
Don't forget your husbands."

"Please welcome Pastor Cowden,
a caring man who loves hurting people."

SEATING SURVEY

Dear Congregant:

Many of you have expressed concern over the seating arrangements in the church. In order for your church office to place you in a seat that will best suit you, please complete the following question-naire and return it to the office.

I would prefer to sit in the:
___ Talking/whispering section
___ No talking section

If talking which subcategory do you prefer?
___ Stock market ___ Sports
___ Aches/pains ___ Gossip

Which of the following would you like to be near so that you might receive free pro-fessional advice?
___ Lawyer ___ Physician
___ Accountant ___ Beautician
___ Stockbroker

I want a seat located:
___ Near my in-laws
___ Far from my in-laws
___ Far from my ex-in-laws

I wish to be seated in a seat where:
___ I can sleep during the preliminaries
___ I can sleep during the sermon
(additional charge)

BULLETIN FILLER

"This. . .is. . .the. . .way. . .the. . .church. . .
sometimes. . .looks. . .to. . .the. . .pastor. . .
when. . .he. . .goes. . .to. . .the. . .pulpit.
BUT
Thechurchwouldlooklikethisifeverybody
broughtsomebodyelsetochurchwiththem."

THE CHURCH DICTIONARY

Amen: The only part of a prayer that
everyone knows.

Bulletin: Information read only during the sermon; Baptist air-conditioning; proof that you attended church.

Choir: A group of people whose singing allows the rest of the congregation to lip-sync.

Hymn: A song of praise, usually sung in a key three octaves higher than the congregation can sing.

Incense: Holy smoke!

Justice: When kids have kids of their own.

Pew: A medieval torture device still found in some old line churches.

Procession: The ceremonial formation at the beginning of many church services, consisting of choir, acolytes, clergy, and late worshipers looking for seats.

Recessional: Same as above going the other direction and led by worshipers trying to beat the crowd to the parking lot.

Ten Commandments: The most important Top Ten list not given by Dave
Letterman.

Ushers: The only people in the congregation who don't know the seating capac-
ity of a pew.

ANOTHER JOB INTERVIEW

Church Office Manager: "How long did
you work at
your other job?"

Job Seeker: "Fifty-five
years."

Church Office Manager: "How old are
you?"

Job Seeker: "Forty-five."

Church Office Manager: "How could you
work fifty-five years when
you are only
forty- five years
old?"

Job Seeker: "Overtime."

JOB DESCRIPTIONS

St. Michael's By the Estuary was getting organized. They had written a mission statement, designed a flow chart, and the office was now working on job descriptions. The following is the first draft.

Senior Pastor
    Is able to leap tall buildings in a single
        bound;
    Is more powerful than a locomotive;
    Is faster than a speeding bullet;
    Walks on water;
    Gives policies to God.

Associate Pastor
    Is able to leap short buildings in a
        single bound;
    Is as powerful as a switch engine;
    Is just as fast as a speeding bullet;
    Walks on water if the sea is calm;
    Talks with God.

Educational Director
> Leaps small buildings with a running
>> start;
> Is almost as powerful as a switch
>> engine;
> Is faster than a speeding BB;
> Walks on water if he knows where the
>> rocks are;
> Talks with God if special request is
>> approved.

Music Director
> Clears a Quonset hut;
> Loses races with a locomotive;
> Can fire a speeding bullet;
> Swims well;
> Is occasionally addressed by God.

Youth Director
> Runs into small buildings;
> Recognizes locomotives two out of
>> three times;
> Used a squirt gun in college;
> Knows how to use the water fountain;
> Mumbles to himself.

Church Secretary
> Lifts buildings to walk under them;
> Kicks locomotives off the track;
> Catches speeding bullets in her teeth;
> When God speaks, she says, "May
>> I ask who's calling?"

MORE BULLETIN BLOOPERS

"Don't let worry kill you—let the church help."

"Bertha Belch, a missionary from Africa, will speak tonight at Calvary Memorial Church in Racine. Come tonight and hear Bertha Belch all the way from Africa."

"The sermon topic for tonight is 'What is Hell?' Come early and listen to the choir warm up."

"Weight Watchers will meet at 7:00 P.M. at First Presbyterian Church. Please use the large double doors at the side entrance."

"Ladies' Bible Study will be held Thursday morning at ten. All ladies are invited to lunch in Fellowship Hall after the B.S. is done."

"Low Self-esteem Support Group to meet Thursday at 7:00 P.M. Please use the back door.

THE CHURCH COMPUTER

Some sage has posted the following over the church secretary's computer:

1. When computing, whatever happens, behave as though you meant it to happen.
2. When you get to the point where you really understand your computer, it's probably obsolete.
3. The first place to look for information is in the section of the manual where you least expect to find it.
4. When the going gets tough—upgrade!

5. For every action, there is an equal and opposite malfunction.
6. To err is human. . .to blame your computer for your mistakes is even more human. It's downright natural!
7. He who laughs last probably made a backup.
8. If at first you don't succeed, blame your computer.
9. A complex system that does not work is invariably found to have evolved from a simpler system that worked just fine.
10. The number one cause of computer problems is computer solutions.
11. A computer program will always do what you tell it to do, but rarely what you want it to do.

STAMP VALUE

Secretary Valerie stopped by the post office to pick up stamps for the church's Christmas mailing.

"What denomination?" asked the clerk.

"Oh, good heavens, have we come to this?" asked Valerie. "Well, let's be ecumenical; give me one hundred Baptist, seventy-five Catholic, fifty Presbyterian, and fifty undecided ones."

FINALLY. . .
A FEW MORE BULLETIN BUNGLES

"Next Sunday is the family hayride and bonfire at the Fosters'. Bring your own hot dogs and guns. Friends are welcome. We'll take care of you."

"Miss Charlene Mason sang 'I Will Not Pass This Way Again,' giving obvious pleasure to the congregation."

"The peacemaking meeting scheduled for today has been canceled due to conflict."

"The sermon this morning is 'Jesus Walks on the Water.' Tonight's sermon is 'Searching for Jesus.'"

"Scouts are saving aluminum cans, bottles, and other items to be recycled. Proceeds will be used to cripple children."

STEWARDSHIP

ROCKIN' THE STEWARD-SHIP

Ever notice all the words that are in the word "Stewardship"? First, there's "Stew." That's what a congregation can get into after a sermon on tithing.

Then there's "war," which is what can take place in a church board discussion of the church budget.

"Ship" is the third syllable. Like the *Titanic*, if there's a hole in church giving, it can sink pretty fast.

Finally the word "hip," a reminder that total stewardship is about the whole body.

MOTIVATION

A little girl became restless as the preacher's sermon dragged on and on. Finally she leaned over to her mother and whispered, "Mommy, if we give him money now, will he let us go?"

PLEDGES

The deacon ran into the pastor's office and exclaimed excitedly, "Pastor, I have terrible news to report! Burglars must've broken in last night. They stole ninety thousand dollars worth of pledges."

WHEN THE "TITHE" COMES IN

Two men were shipwrecked on a desert island. One was churchgoer and the other wasn't. The minute they arrived on the island, the non-churchgoer began screaming and yelling, "We're going to die! There's no food! No water! We're going to die!"

The other man was calmly propped against a palm tree, which drove the other guy crazy. "Don't you understand? We're going to die! What's wrong with you?"

"You don't understand," said the churchgoer, "I make one hundred thousand dollars a week."

"What difference does that make?" asked the non-churchgoer. "We're on a desert island. We're going to die."

The churchgoer smiled, "You just don't get it. I make one hundred thousand dollars a week, and I tithe. My pastor will find me!"

How to Kill Your Pastor

A minister was asked to inform a man with a heart condition that he had just inherited a million dollars. Everyone was afraid the shock would cause a heart attack and the man would die.

The minister went to the man's house and said, "Joe, what would you do if you inherited a million dollars?"

Joe responded, "Well, Pastor, I think I would give half of it to the church."

And the minister fell over dead.

Ouch!

"I'll give till it hurts," said a member of Hope Church to his pastor, "but you need to know I'm terribly sensitive to pain."

Too frequently an anonymous gift to the church is a donation by someone who hopes everyone will find out without his telling them.

If you want to know about the troubles the church is having, ask someone who hasn't been there for months.

FUND-RAISING

Pastor Martin led off the special fund-raising drive by visiting the James's home, where Tim responded to his pastor's request for a hundred dollars with, "No, Pastor, I can't do it."

"Well then, how about fifty?"

"I can't do it, Pastor, I'm heavily in debt, and I have to pay my creditors first."

"But, Tim, you owe a great debt to God, too. Don't you think he deserves your input?"

"He sure does, Pastor, but God isn't crowding me like my other creditors are."

COUGH IT UP

Mother: "Quick, Henry, call the doctor. Johnny just swallowed a nickel."

Father: "I think we ought to send for the minister. He can get money out of anybody."

GETTING PLASTERED

The dilapidated old church building desperately needed remodeling. So the pastor made an impassioned appeal from his pulpit—looking directly at Brother Goldman, the richest man in town. In the middle of his plea, a slab of plaster fell from the ceiling and struck the rich man on the shoulder. He quickly jumped to his feet and shouted, "Pastor, I will increase my donation to five thousand dollars."

Before he could sit down again, another slab fell and hit him, then another and another. Finally Goldman screamed at the top of his lungs, "Pastor, I will double my pledge." Then he sat down, just as a larger chunk of plaster fell and hit him on the head, forcing him to stand again and holler, "Pastor, I will give fifty thousand dollars!"

This prompted Deacon Phillips to shout, "Hit him again, Lord! Hit him again!"

CURRENCY GOES TO CHURCH

A well-worn one dollar bill and a similarly distressed twenty dollar bill arrive at the Federal Reserve Bank to be retired. As they move along the conveyer belt to be burned, they strike up a conversation.

The twenty reminisces about its travels all over the country. "I've had a pretty good life," it proclaims. "Why I've been to Las Vegas and Atlantic City, performances on Broadway, the best restaurants in New York, even a cruise to the Caribbean."

"Wow!" exclaims the one dollar bill. "You've really had an exciting life!"

"So tell me," says the twenty, "where

have you been throughout your lifetime?"

The one dollar bill replies, "Oh, I've been to the Methodist Church, the Baptist Church, the Lutheran Church. . ."

"Tell me," the twenty dollar bill interrupts, "what's a church?"

DIRECT APPROACH

Pastor Dixon had a problem; he had to ask the congregation to pledge more money for church repairs than they anticipated. On his way to the chancel, he asked the organist to be ready to play something suitable for the pledging. At the appropriate time, Pastor Dixon announced, "Brothers and sisters, we are in great difficulty. Our roof repairs have run five thousand dollars over the estimated cost. That means we must raise that amount this morning. Any of you who are willing to increase your original pledge, please stand up."

At that very moment the organist tore into "The Star Spangled Banner."

And the whole congregation stood.

THE BENEFITS OF GIVING

The Grace Church treasurer went to the pastor with the bad news that they couldn't make the mortgage payment or pay the utilities. So the pastor went to his congregation on Sunday morning. "We need an extra large offering this morning." Then he added, "We will honor the person who gives the largest offering by inviting him or her to pick out three hymns for the service."

To the Pastor's delight, there was a one thousand dollar bill in the plate, which made him so excited he asked the big giver to identify himself so he could say "thank you."

A quiet little lady sitting in the back corner shyly stood, and the pastor invited her to the front. Telling her how generous her gift was, he also invited her to select three hymns. Her eyes brightened as she looked over the congregation, pointed to the three handsomest men in the sanctuary, and said, "I'll take him and him and him."

WORLDLY WEALTH

A rich man was near death. He was grieved because he'd worked so hard for his money, and he wanted to be able to take it to heaven. An angel heard his concern and appeared to him. "Sorry, but you can't take your wealth with you."

The man pled with the angel.

Later the angel reappeared and told the wealthy man that he could take one suitcase with him. Overjoyed, the man found his largest valise and filled it with gold bars.

When he finally died and showed up in heaven, St. Peter saw the suitcase and said, "Hold on, you can't bring that in here."

The man explained to St. Peter that he had permission. Sure enough, the saint checked the record and verified the man's story. "But," St. Peter added, "I am supposed to check the contents before letting it through."

So St. Peter opened the suitcase to discover what was too precious to leave behind. He couldn't believe his eyes. "You brought pavement?"

Fair Is Fair

Hank: "God, I was wondering, how long is a million years to you?"

God: "Son, a million years is like a second to me."

Hank: "God, how much is a million dollars to you?"

God: "Son, a million dollars to me is like one penny to you."

Hank: "God, can I have one of your pennies?"

God: "Just a second, son."

More On Tithing

A rather stingy man died and went to heaven. He was met at the front gate by St. Peter, who led him on a house tour down the golden streets. They passed mansion after beautiful mansion until they came to the end of the street and stopped in front of a tiny shack without gold paving in front. "And here is where you will be living, sir," Peter announced.

"Me live here?" the stingy man yelled. "How come?"

Peter replied, "I did the best I could with the money you sent us."

CHEERFUL GIVER

On Sunday morning a father gave his son a couple of quarters and a dollar. "Put the dollar in the offering," the father said, "then you can have the fifty cents for ice cream."

When the boy came home, he still had his dollar. "Why didn't you put the dollar in the offering?" his father asked.

"Well, it was like this," the boy explained. "The preacher said that God loves a cheerful giver. I could give the fifty cents a whole lot more cheerfully than I could the dollar."

OFFERTORY STATEMENTS

"The Lord owns the cattle on a thousand hills. He only needs cowboys to round them up. Will the ushers please come forward for the offering?"

"Let us give generously—according to what you reported on your income tax."

"Give now, before the cost of living goes up more, and you can't afford to. Amen"

"As you give this morning, remember that many of our ambitions are nipped in the budget."

"Not only is it more blessed to give than to receive, but it's also tax deductible."

"The Lord loveth a cheerful giver. . .but He also accepts from a grouch."

"Do you give to the Lord's work weekly— or weakly?"

"If you are stupid enough to make money your god, it'll bother you like the devil."

"All people should try to spend their lives doing things that will outlast them."

"Support your church. You can't take your money with you, but you can send it on ahead."

"Money doesn't go as far as it used to, but at least it goes faster."

PROFIT SHARING

Gigi and her husband taught first grade Sunday school at their affluent suburban church. For several weeks they had studied the Old Testament prophets. Before moving on to Jeremiah, Gigi asked the children if they remembered what a prophet is.

Daughter Natalie was the only child to raise her hand. Gigi beamed. *My angel has listened and remembered,* she thought.

"Now, Natalie, tell us what a prophet is."

Little Natalie stood proudly and announced, "A prophet is when you make more money than you can spend."

OVERDRAWN

Newly-married pastor: "Honey, I just got a notice from the bank saying I'm overdrawn."

Newly-wed wife: "Try some other bank. They can't all be overdrawn."

DEDUCTIONS

A little boy who wanted one hundred dollars very much prayed and prayed for two weeks, but nothing happened. Then he decided to write a letter to God requesting the one hundred dollars.

When the post office received the letter addressed to "God, USA," they didn't know what to do with it, so sent it the president at the White House. The president was so impressed he instructed his secretary to send the little boy a five dollar bill. "That should look like a large sum of money to one so young."

The boy was delighted with the five dollars and immediately sat down to write a thank-you note to God, which read, "Dear God, thank you for sending me the money. However, I notice that for some reason you had it sent through Washington D. C., and as usual, the government deducted ninety-five percent."

GOOD NEWS, BAD NEWS

The pastor of Second Church stood before his congregation and announced, "I have bad news, I have good news, and I have bad news."

"The bad news is, the church needs a new roof!" The congregation groaned.

"The good news is, we have enough

money for the new roof." A cheer went up from the congregation.

"The bad news is, it's still in your pockets."

FAITHFUL WITH MUCH

At a Wednesday evening church meeting a very wealthy man rose to give his testimony. "I'm a millionaire," he said, "and I attribute it all to the rich blessings of God in my life. I can still remember the turning point in my faith.

"I had just earned my first dollar, and I went to a church meeting that night. The speaker was a missionary who told about his work. I knew that I only had a dollar bill and had either to give it all to God's work or nothing at all. So at that moment I decided to give my whole dollar to God. I believe that's why I'm a millionaire today."

As he finished it was clear that everyone was moved by the man's story. As he took his seat, a little old lady sitting in the same pew leaned over and said, "Wonderful story! I dare you to do it again!"

DEAR PASTOR. . .

"I'm sorry I can't put more money in the plate, but my father didn't give me a raise in my allowance. Could you have a sermon about a raise in a kid's allowance?"

Patty, age ten

"I liked your sermon where you said that good health is more important than money, but I still want a raise in my allowance."

Eleanor, age twelve

"Please say in your sermon that Peter Peterson has been a good boy all week, and that he ought to have a bigger allowance. I am Peter Peterson."

Pete, age nine

"My father ought to be a minister. Every day he gives us a sermon about money."

Robert, age eleven

For the Bulletin

"Tithe if you love Jesus. Anyone can honk."

"The wages of sin is death. Repent before payday."

"Worry is interest paid on trouble before it is due."

"You can give without loving, but you can't love without giving."

Top Reasons to Tithe

1. Your church started a new stewardship drive—every time you give, your chance of winning increases.
2. There's no money for new choir robes, so the choir has started wearing their bathrobes during the service.
3. The last few Sundays the treasurer has gotten up halfway through the service and turned the heat/air conditioning off.

4. The preacher's wife has worn the same dress every Sunday for the past three years.
5. The ushers are starting to drool and growl as they collect the offering.
6. The offering plates have been sold and replaced with ice cream buckets.
7. The treasurer has started wearing sackcloth and ashes.
8. You can't call the church office because the phone has been disconnected.
9. Parking meters have been installed in the church parking lot.

And the most important reason. . .

10. As a Christian church member, you understand the privilege it is to have a partnership in the gospel! (See Malachi 3:8–10.)

BODY STEWARDSHIP

During a special total stewardship emphasis at a church in Oak Harbor, Washington, the following was taped to the mirrors in both the men's and women's rest rooms:

> *Lord, my soul is ripped with riot,*
> *Incited by my wicked diet.*

"We are what we eat," said a wise old man.
"Lord, if that's true, I'm a garbage can.
I want to rise on Judgment Day,
    that's plain,
But at my present weight I'll need a crane.
So grant me strength that I may not fall
Into the clutches of cholesterol.
May my flesh with carrot curls be sated,
That my soul may be polyunsaturated.
And show me the light that I might
    bear witness
To the President's Council on Physical
    Fitness.
And oleo margarine I'll never mutter,
For the road to h*** is spread with butter.
And cream is cursed, and cake is awful,
And Satan is hiding in every waffle.
Mephistopheles lurks in provolone;
The devil is in each slice of bologna.
Beelzebub is a chocolate drop,

And Lucifer is a lollipop.
Give me this day my daily slice,
But cut it thin and toast it twice.
I beg upon my dimpled knees,
Deliver me from jujubes.
And when my days of trial are done,
And my war with malted milks is won,
Let me stand with saints in heaven,
In a shining robe, size 37!
I can do it, Lord, if you'll show to me
The virtues of lettuce and celery.
If you'll teach me the evil of mayonnaise,
The sinfulness of hollandaise
And pasta Milanese,
And potatoes a la lyonnaise
And crisp fried chicken from the south,
Lord, if you love me, shut my mouth."

SPECIAL DAYS

Red letter days at church are excuses to have fun. Pot luck dinners abound, the pastor actually stands in his pulpit and announces a Shrove Tuesday Pancake Griddle Toss with a straight face (while the bulletin declared it a "girdle" toss), and the annual "Date with a Saint" on All Saints Day brought palpitations of anticipation from the Older Ladies' Bible class.

Sit back and revel in this humor of the seasons. And season well with equal parts of snickers, sniggers, guffaws, and quiet smiles of recognition.

NO EXCUSE SUNDAY

To make it possible for everyone to attend church next Sunday, we are going to have a special "No Excuse Sunday."

Cots will be placed in the foyer for those who say "Sunday is my only day to sleep in."

There will be a special section with lounge chairs for those who feel that our pews are too hard.

We will have steel helmets for those who say, "The roof would cave in if I ever came to church."

Relatives and friends will be in attendance for those who can't go to church and cook dinner too.

Doctors and nurses will be in attendance for those who plan to be sick on Sunday.

The sanctuary will be decorated with both Christmas poinsettias and Easter lilies for those who have never seen the church without them.

WIFE APPRECIATION SUNDAY (TONGUE IN CHEEK)

Adam was walking around the Garden of Eden feeling very lonely, causing God to ask, "What's wrong with you, Adam?" Adam replied that he didn't have anyone to talk to. So God announced that he was going to give him a companion—a woman.

"A woman?" Adam replied.

Then God described her, "She will be someone to cook for you and wash your clothes. She will always agree with every decision you make. She will bear your children and never ask you to get up in the middle of the night to care for them. This woman will not nag you and will always be the first to admit when she is wrong. She will never have a headache and will freely give you love and compassion whenever you need it."

"What is she going to cost me, God?" Adam asked.

"An arm and a leg," God responded.

Adam thought a moment and asked, "What can I get for just a rib?"

The rest is history.

FOR MOTHER'S DAY

You know you're a mother when you're up each night until 10:00 P.M., vacuuming, dusting, wiping, washing, drying, loading, unloading, shopping, cooking, driving, flushing, ironing, sweeping, picking up, changing sheets, changing diapers, bathing, helping with homework, paying bills, budgeting, clipping coupons, folding clothes, putting to bed, dragging out of bed, brushing, chasing, buckling, feeding, swinging, playing ball, bike riding, pushing trucks, cuddling dolls, roller blading, catching, blowing bubbles, running sprinklers, sliding, taking walks, coloring, crafting, jumping rope, raking, trimming, planting, edging, mowing, gardening, painting, and walking/feeding the dog. You get up at 5:30 A.M., and you have no time to eat, sleep, drink, or go to the bathroom, and yet—you still manage to gain ten pounds.

MOTHER'S DAY TEA

Pastor Smith has been asked to say a few words about mothers at the annual Mother's Day tea. His wife is coaching him on proper tea manners.

Wife: "George, you have such atrocious
       tea table manners."
Pastor: "You're supposed to stick your little
       finger out when you drink tea."
Wife: "With the tea bag hanging from it?"

THEIR MOTHERS MAY HAVE SAID IT

"Sampson! Get your hand out of that lion.
You don't know where it's been!"

"David! I told you not to play in the house
with that sling! Go practice your harp. We
pay good money for those lessons."

"Abraham! Stop wandering around the
countryside and get home for supper."

"Shadrach, Meshach, and Abednego!
I told you never to play with fire!"

"Cain! Get off your brother! You're going
to kill him some day!"

"Noah! No, you can't keep them! How many times do I have to tell you, don't bring home any more strays."

"Gideon! Have you been hiding in that winepress again? Look at your clothes."

"James and John! No more burping contests at the dinner table, please. People are going to call you the sons of thunder."

"Judas! Have you been in my purse again?"

"Jesus! Be careful with those tools; You don't want to put a nail through your finger."

FIREWORKS

The annual Fourth of July picnic and fireworks sponsored by First Baptist is one of the highlights of the church year. Last year's pyrotechnic show will not be forgotten by all those standing around Donnie Walker on his father's shoulders. When the last ball of fire streaked across the sky and the audience was cheering, little Donnie kept looking up into the sky and saying, "Thank you, God."

JESUS IS BETTER THAN SANTA

Santa lives at the North Pole; Jesus is everywhere.

Santa rides in a sleigh; Jesus rides on the wind and walks on the water.

Santa comes but once a year; Jesus is an ever present help.

Santa comes down your chimney uninvited; Jesus stands at your door and knocks.

Santa makes you stand in line to see him; Jesus is as close as the mention of His name.

Santa lets you sit on his lap; Jesus lets you rest in His arms.

Santa asks, "Little boy, little girl, what is your name?" Jesus knew our names before we did.

Santa has a belly like a bowl full of jelly; Jesus has a heart full of love.

Santa offers "Ho, ho, ho"; Jesus offers health, help, and hope.

Santa says "You better not cry"; Jesus says, "Cast all your cares on me for I care for you."

Santa's little helpers make toys; Jesus makes new lives, mends hearts, repairs broken homes.

Santa may make you chuckle; Jesus gives you joy.

Santa puts gifts under your tree; Jesus became our gift and died on the tree.

There's really no comparison. Jesus is the reason for the season.

THREE WISE WOMEN

You do know what would have happened if it had been three wise women instead of men, don't you? They would have asked for directions, arrived on time, helped deliver the baby, cleaned the stable, made

a casserole, and brought disposable diapers
as a gifts!

THE ADVENT WREATH

Four weeks before Christmas, Reverend
Johnson of Christ Lutheran was leading a
children's service featuring an Advent
wreath. He had told them what the three
purple candles represented, then asked,
"Does anyone know what the pink one
means?" No one answered.

Finally little Sara's hand went up. "Are
they expecting a girl?"

CHRISTMAS NUTS

A pastor got this note accompanying a box
of Christmas goodies, addressed to him and
his wife, from elderly Sister Rose Mary.

Dear Pastor,
Knowing that you do not eat sweets,
I am sending the candy to your wife—
and nuts to you.

LITTLE RED WAGON

It was the day after Christmas at a down-town church in San Francisco. The pastor was out in front looking over the manger scene set up on the front lawn when he noticed the Christ Child figure was missing.

Right on cue, he turned to see a little boy with a red wagon coming down the street and in the wagon was the figure of the infant Jesus. So the pastor walked up to the boy and asked, "Well, young man, where did you pick up your passenger?"

"I got Him here, from the church."

"And why did you take Him?"

The little boy replied, "Well, about a week before Christmas I prayed to the little Lord Jesus, and I told Him if He would bring me a red wagon for Christmas, I would give Him a ride around the block in it."

NATIVITY FIRE

A rural church began the lovely Christmas tradition of staging a Living Nativity scene on the front lawn. It became the talk of that small community. A visitor driving through town stopped and admired the performance, but one feature troubled him. The three wise men were carrying heavy canvas hoses, and they wore fire helmets. Unable to come up with an explanation on his own, the tourist went to one of the church members who stood by.

"Why the fire hoses and helmets on the three wise men?" he asked.

The church lady shook her head in disgust and replied, "You Yankees never do read the Bible!"

He assured her he did, but couldn't recall anything about firemen in the Bible.

The lady indignantly pulled her Bible out from under her arm and riffled through the pages, finally jabbing her finger at one particular passage. Putting the Good Book right up in his face she said, "See, Yankee, it says right here, 'The three wise men came from afar. . .'"

YOUTH SUNDAY

As a special Youth Week project, Ted Montgomery of Campus United Methodist asked his university group to list ways the Bible may have been different if it had been written by fellow students. These are a few they came up with:

Loaves and fishes would have been replaced by pizza and chips.

Ten Commandments are actually five, but because they are double-spaced and written in a large font, they look like ten.

Forbidden fruit would have been eaten only because it wasn't dining hall food.

Paul's letter to the Romans would become Paul's E-mail to the Romans.

Reason Cain killed Abel—they were roommates.

Place where the end of the world occurs—not the Plains of Armageddon, but Finals.

Reason why Moses and followers wandered in the desert for forty years—they didn't want to ask directions and look like freshmen.

Tower of Babel blamed for foreign language requirement.

Instead of creating the world in six days and resting on the seventh, God would have put it off until the night before it was due and then pulled an all-nighter and hoped no one noticed.

GRANDPARENTS' SUNDAY

A little girl sat on her grandfather's lap as he read her a bedtime story. From time to time, she'd reach up and touch his wrinkled cheek. Then she'd touch her own cheek thoughtfully.

Finally she spoke, "Grandpa, did God make you?"

"Yes, sweetheart," he answered. "God made me a long time ago."

"Did God make me, too?" she asked.

"Yes, indeed, honey," he answered. "God made you just a little while ago."

She touched his face again, and then her own.

"He's getting better at it, isn't He?" she asked.

For Super Bowl Sunday

"Quarterback Sneak"—Church members quietly leaving during the invitation.

"Draw Play"—What many children do with their bulletins during worship.

"Halftime"—The period between Sunday school and worship when many choose to leave.

"Benchwarmer"—Those who do not sing, pray, work, or apparently do anything.

"Backfield-in-Motion"—Making a trip up the aisle to the back (rest room or water fountain) during the service.

"Staying in the Pocket"—What happens to a lot of money that should be given to the Lord's work.

"Two-minute Warning"—The point at which you realize the sermon is almost over and begin to gather up your belongings.

"Instant Replay"—The preacher misplaces his notes and falls back on last Sunday's illustrations.

"Sudden Death"—What happens to the congregation's attention span if the preacher goes overtime.

"Trap"—You are called on to pray, and your mind is a million miles away.

"End Run"—Getting out of church fast by skirting around behind the pastor at the door.

"Flex Defense"—The ability to allow absolutely nothing during the sermon to affect your life.

"Halfback Option"—The decision of fifty percent of the congregation not to return for the evening service.

"Blitz"—The rush for restaurants following the benediction.

WEDDING DAY

Little Tony was in his uncle's wedding. As he came down the aisle during the ceremony, he carefully took two steps, then stopped and turned to the crowd. When facing the congregation he put his hands up like claws and roared loudly. So it went, step, step, turn, roar, step, step, turn, roar, all the way down the aisle.

As you can imagine, the congregation was near tears from laughing. By the time little Tony reached the altar, he was near tears too. When later asked what he was doing, the boy sniffed and said, "I was being the Ring Bear."

Vows

"Do you take this woman for your wedded wife," the minister asked the nervous bridegroom. "For better or worse, for richer, for poorer, in sickness or. . ."

"Just a minute, Pastor!" interrupted the bride. "Stop now or you'll talk him right out of it."

Marriage Offer

Reverend Walker was scheduled to perform a special wedding ceremony immediately following the Sunday morning service. He planned to perform the rite before the entire congregation, but for the life of him, he could not remember the names of the two members whom he was to marry. He got around his dilemma this way: "Will those who want to get married now, please come stand before me."

At once, six single ladies, four widows, and five single men stood, went to the aisle, and walked to the front.

OLD TIMERS' SUNDAY

First Baptist has instigated a summer special day—Old Timers' Sunday. This year farmer John Calver brought in his horse and carriage with a hand-lettered sign: "Energy efficient vehicle. Runs on oats and grass. Caution: Do not step in exhaust."

THE MUSIC DEPARTMENT

"If music be the food of love, play on," said the Bard of Avon (Shakespeare to the uninitiated), and somebody once said, "Music hath charms to soothe the savage beast," causing the pastor of First Baptist to exclaim, "That 'somebody' doesn't know my choir!"

Probably not, but pray next Sunday's bulletin doesn't carry this notice. "Mrs. Smith will sink two numbers. She will be accompanied by the choir."

While sacred music is nothing to laugh at, those who produce it can be worth a snicker or two.

HYMN PROFESSIONS

Here's an old standby that's worth sharing with a music director.

Dentist's hymn—"Crown Him With Many Crowns"

Mender's hymn—"Holy, Holy, Holy"

Politician's hymn—"Standing on the Promises"

Shopper's hymn—"In the Sweet By and By"

Paramedic's hymn—"Revive Us Again"

Shoe repairer's hymn—"It Is Well with My Soul"

Librarian's hymn—"Whispering Hope"

Umpire's hymn—"I Need No Other Argument"

Golfer's hymn—"There Is a Green Hill Far Away"

IRS agent's hymn—"I Surrender All"

Gossip's hymn—"Pass It On"

Psychiatrist's hymn—"Just a Little Talk With Jesus"

Haberdasher's hymn—"Blest Be the Tie"

Dot-com sales hymn—"A Charge to Keep I Have"

There's a zillion more.

GOD'S NAME

A "pillar of the church" passed away and was on his way to heaven. When he got to the pearly gates of heaven, he met an angel. The angel asked him what God's name was.

"Oh, that's easy," the man replied. "His name is Andy."

"What makes you think his name is Andy?" the angel asked.

"Well, you see at church we used to sing this song, 'Andy walks with me, Andy talks with me.'"

CARTOON CUTLINE

Unhappy pastor and his frustrated church bell ringer are standing in the steeple, and the minister is explaining, "No, no, Higby. It's ding before dong except after bong."

MELLOW

The church baritone soloist was delighted

when one of the members spoke to him after service and said, "You have a very mellow voice."

When he got home, he went directly to his dictionary and discovered the meaning of "mellow." He read, "Mellow: overripe and almost rotten."

POOR SINGING

At the close of the service a visiting preacher remarked to the minister that he thought the singing was terribly poor and asked what the problem was. The home-team minister replied, "Yes, unfortunately the agnostics here are dreadful."

A LIMERICK

There was a young girl in the choir
Whose voice went up higher and higher,
Till one Sunday night
It vanished from sight,
And turned up next day in the spire.

NOTHING BUT THE TRUTH

High soprano Karen Phillips once sang in the choir, but for several services she was in the congregation and not in the loft. When asked why she no longer sang, she explained, "One Sunday when I was home sick with a cold, several folks asked if the organ had been repaired."

PREACHER VS. MUSIC LEADER

There was a church where the preacher and the minister of music were not getting along. As time went by, this spirit began to spill over into the worship service.

The first week the preacher preached on commitment and how we should all dedicate ourselves to God. The music director led the song, "I Shall Not Be Moved."

The second week the preacher preached on tithing and how we all should gladly give to the work of the Lord. The director led the song, "Jesus Paid It All."

The third week the preacher preached on gossiping and how we should all watch our tongues. The music director led, "I Love to Tell the Story."

With all this going on, the preacher became totally disgusted over the situation and the following Sunday told the congregation that he was considering resigning. The music director led, "Oh, Why Not Tonight."

As it came to pass, the preacher did resign. The next week he informed the church that it was Jesus who led him there and it was Jesus who was taking him away. The music leader led the song, "What a Friend We Have in Jesus."

ORGANIST

Back in the days when the church janitor had to pump air into the pipe organ to make it work, Eloise, the new organist, dearly wanted to make an impression on the visiting clergyman with her playing.

She wrote a note to the old janitor who had been slack in pumping the organ air and handed it to him just before the service started. But, making a natural mistake, the janitor passed the note on to the visiting preacher, who opened it and read, "Keep blowing away until I give you the signal to stop."

VOCAL CLAIMS

With a booming voice, the Minister of Music bragged to his congregation, "Two years ago I insured my voice with Lloyd's of London for 750,000 dollars."

The crowded sanctuary was hushed. Suddenly an elderly woman spoke out. "So," she said, "what did you do with the money?"

GET MEN IN THE CHOIR

The top ten reasons why men need to join the choir:
1. Rehearsals are every Wednesday night.

Which means that for those few hours you can significantly reduce your risk of getting tendinitis from nonstop clicking of a TV remote control or computer mouse.

2. Because you wear a choir robe, you are liberated from the less than manly task of coordinating your Sunday wardrobe.

3. From your special vantage point, looking over the entire congregation, you can play a little game of "Who's Sleeping and Who's Praying?"

4. On the other hand, sitting in view of a sanctuary full of people on a weekly basis makes it much less likely you yourself will give in to a chronic loss of sleep—although it's been known to happen.

5. If you think your singing in the shower sounds good, wait until you've sung with us for a few weeks.

6. Singing in a choir is one of the few activities for me that doesn't require electronic equipment or expensive power tools.

7. For the fitness buffs, singing in the choir is not only heart healthy, it's soul healthy. There are no monthly membership fees, and it's a lot easier on the knees than jogging.

8. If you think you've already done everything there is to do and there are no extreme challenges left, try staying on pitch with our tenors and basses.

9. Choir rehearsals last half as long as a professional football game, but is at least twice as satisfying. No rehearsals on Monday night.

10. When people ask you whether you've been behaving yourself, you can say with the utmost sincerity, "Hey, I'm a choir boy."

FUND-RAISING

The church choir was putting on a car wash to raise money for their annual tour. They made a large sign which read, "Car Wash for Choir Trip."

On the given Saturday, business was terrific, but by two o'clock the skies clouded and the rain poured, and there were hardly any customers.

Finally one of the girl washers had an idea. She printed a large cardboard poster which read, "We Wash and God Rinses." Business boomed!

HONEST HYMNS

There are people who in their honest moments, ought to sing these familiar hymns as indicated.

"I Surrender Some"
"There Shall Be Sprinkles of
    Blessings"
"Fill My Spoon, Lord"
"Oh, How I Like Jesus"
"When the Saints Go Sneaking In"
"I Love to Talk about Telling the
    Story"
"Take My Life and Let Me Be"

"Onward Christian Reservists"
"Where He Leads Me, I Will Think
about Following"
"Just As I Make Believe I Am"

FROM THE MOUTHS OF CHURCH MEMBERS

Pianist: "Are you fond of music?"
Communicant: "Yes, but keep right on
                  playing."

DOGGONE GOOD

Little Jason was practicing his violin to
play a solo in church, and the torturous
noise was making the dog howl. Upstairs,
the boy's father was trying to work. After
trying to put up with the combined racket
of the violin and the dog for twenty
minutes, the father finally called down,
"Jason. Can't you play something the dog
doesn't know?"

KIDS

Art Linkletter wasn't off his form when he used to exclaim, "Kids say the darndest things." They also write, draw, perceive, and react in the darndest ways, too.

Kid humor is some of the brightest and funniest. All the classic joke books are crammed with juvenile funnies. Why? Because they don't know they're being cute. Truth is, don't call them the church of tomorrow; they are a part of the church today!

FOR WHOM THE BELL. . .

A minister is walking down the street one sunny afternoon when he notices a very small boy trying to press a doorbell on a house across the street. But the doorbell is too high for the little boy to reach.

After watching the boy's efforts, the minister decides to give the lad a hand. So he crosses over and goes up to the house and gives the bell a solid ring.

Crouching down to the little boy's level, the minister smiles benevolently and asks, "And now what, my little man?"

To which the boy replies, "Now we run!"

CARTOON CUTLINE

A family is greeting their pastor after the service. Junior looks up and declares, "My dad says my mom is a pagan because she serves burnt offerings for dinner."

THE CONFESSIONAL

One day a boy and his grandparents came to visit a 150-year-old historic Catholic church. As they toured the church, the grandfather explained the reason for some of the architectural and liturgical features, while the boy listened intently. Then they reached the confessional in the back.

"I know what this is!" the boy enthused, "It's for time-out, right?"

OUCH!

After a Sunday morning church service, Philip suddenly announced to his mother, "Mom, I've decided to become a minister when I grow up."

"That's okay with me. But what made you decide that?"

"Well," said the little boy, "I'll have to go to church on Sunday anyway, so I figure it will be more fun to stand up and yell, than to sit down and listen."

FACES

Watching Sunday school pupil Willy making faces at the kids around him, teacher Miss Betsy stopped the lesson and said, "Willy, when I was your age, I was told that that if I made ugly faces, my face would freeze that way."

Bobby looked up and replied innocently, "Well, Miss Betsy, you can't say you weren't warned."

A LETTER

A Sunday school teacher challenged her children to take some time on Sunday afternoon to write a letter to God. They were to bring their letters back the following Sunday. One little boy, Benny, wrote, "Dear God, We had a good time at church today. Wish you could have been there."

PARTISANSHIP

A little girl from Minneapolis came home from church with a frown. "I'm not going back there anymore," she announced. "I don't like the Bible they use in Sunday school."

"Why not?" asked her astonished mother.

"Because," the little girl declared, "the Bible they use is always talking about St. Paul, and it never once mentions Minneapolis."

GLORIA PATRIA

While walking up the front lane to his house, Pastor Norris of First Church heard the intoning of a prayer that nearly wilted his collar. His five-year-old son and his playmates had found a dead bird and were giving it a Christian funeral. The burial spot was dug, and the minister's son was selected to say the appropriate prayer. So, with dignity he intoned his version of what he thought his father always said, "Glory be to the Faaaather, and to the Sonnnn. . . and into the hole you gooo."

COME IN

An exasperated mother, whose son was always getting into mischief, finally asked him, "Tommy, how do you expect to get into heaven someday?"

The boy thought it over and explained, "Well, I'll just run in and out and in and out and keep slamming the gate until St. Peter says, 'For heaven's sake, Tommy, come in or stay out.'"

RIGHT AND WRONG

A Sunday school teacher was teaching her class about the difference between right and wrong.

"All right, children, let's take another example," she said. "If I were to get into a man's pocket and take his billfold with all his money, what would I be?"

Little Harold, the pastor's son, raised his hand, and with a confident smile, he blurted out, "You'd be his wife!"

OT Q's & A's

Each week at St. John's church, children in the service are invited to submit "Stump the Pastor" questions and answers. Here's a sampling.

Q. Who was the greatest financier in the Bible?

A. Noah. He was floating his stock while everyone else was in liquidation.

Q. Who was the greatest female financier
in the Bible?
A. Pharaoh's daughter. She went down to
the bank of the Nile and drew out a
little prophet.

Q. How did Adam and Eve feel when
expelled from the Garden of Eden?
A. They were really put out.

Q. What excuse did Adam give to his
children as to why he no longer lived
in Eden?
A. Your mother ate us out of house and
home.

KNIFE 'N FORK

The Kelly family invited their pastor and
wife to dinner, and it was little Tyler's job
to set the table. When it came time to eat,
Tyler's mother asked with surprise, "Why
didn't you give Mrs. Brown any silverware,
dear?"

"I didn't think I needed to," Tyler explained, "I heard Daddy say she always eats like a horse."

EATING GOAT

A young couple invited their pastor for Sunday dinner. While they were in the kitchen preparing the meal, their young son was in the living room entertaining the pastor.

"What are we having for dinner?" the minister asked.

"Goat," replied the boy.

"Goat?" repeated the startled pastor. "Are you sure about that?"

"Yep," said the youngster. "I heard Dad tell Mom, 'Might as well have the old goat for dinner today as any other day.'"

SHE DID?

Mrs. Smith and her little daughter Betty were outside the church watching all the comings and goings of a wedding. After it was over, Betty asked her mother, "Why did the bride change her mind?"

"What do you mean, 'change her mind'?" asked Mrs. Smith.

"Well," said Betty, "she went into the church with one man and came out with another."

THE CHILDREN'S SERMON

Sister Smith invited the children to come forward around the altar for an object lesson using squirrels as an example of industry and planning ahead. She requested that the boys and girls raise their hands when they knew what she was describing.

"This thing lives in trees [pause] and eats nuts [pause]." No hands went up. "It is gray [pause] and has a long bushy tail [pause]." The children looked at each other, but no hands were raised. "And it jumps from branch to branch [pause] and chatters when it gets excited [pause]."

Finally a little boy tentatively raised his hand. Sister Smith breathed a sigh of relief and called on him. "Well," he said, "I know the answer must be Jesus, but it sure sounds more like a squirrel to me."

THE VERGE

A Sunday school teacher asked her class, "What was Jesus' mother's name?"

Little Susan answered, "Mary."

The teacher then asked, "And who knows what Jesus' father's name was?"

Little Burt called out, "The Verge."

Confused, the teacher asked, "Where did you get that, Burt?"

The little boy smiled and responded, "Well, you know they are always talking about 'the Verge 'n Mary.'"

GOD THE ARTIST

Bobby and his grandmother were looking at vacation pictures. "It looks just like an artist painted this scenery," Grandma said. "Did you know God painted it all for you, Bobby?"

"Yes," Bobby said. "God did it with His left hand."

This confused his grandmother a bit, "What makes you say God did this with His left hand?"

"Well," said Bobby, "we learned at Sunday school last week that Jesus sits on God's right hand."

BRAINWASHING

The Johnson family with their five-year-old daughter sat close to the front at church so little Annie could see the whole service. Since they were attending an Episcopal Church, on this particular Sunday the minister was baptizing a tiny infant.

Annie Johnson was quite taken with the ritual, especially when the minister poured water over the baby's head. With a quizzical look, the little girl turned to her father and with a loud voice asked, "Daddy, why are they brainwashing that baby?"

CRITICS

When the family returned from Sunday morning service, the father criticized the sermon, the soloist, the organist, and just about everything else. But the subject was quickly dropped when junior piped up, "But it was pretty good for a quarter, don't you think, Dad?"

WHERE JESUS IS

Four-year-old Brianna was at the pediatrician for a check up. When the doctor looked in her ears, he asked, "Do you think I'll find Big Bird in here?" Brianna only giggled.

Next, the doctor took a tongue depressor and looked down her throat. This time he asked, "Do you think I'll find the Cookie Monster down there?" Brianna giggled again.

Then the doctor put a stethoscope to her chest. As he listened to her heartbeat, he asked, "Do you think I'll hear Barney in there?"

"Oh, no!" Brianna replied. "Jesus is in my heart. Barney's on my underpants."

"GOD TELLS ME"

Churchman Bill Keane, creator of the popular "Family Circus" comic strip, tells of a time when he was penciling-in one of his cartoons and his son Jeffy asked, "Daddy, how do you know what to draw?"

Keane answered, "God tells me."

Then Jeffy innocently responded, "Then why do you keep erasing parts of it?"

THE CHRISTENING

After the christening of his baby brother in church, little Johnny sobbed all the way home in the back seat of the car. His father asked him three times what was wrong. Finally the boy replied, "That pastor said he wanted us brought up in a Christian home, and I want to stay with you guys!"

AFRAID OF THE DARK

One of Tommy's favorite games was to ride his mother's broom around the yard like a horse. When it started to get dark, Tommy went into the house, leaving the broom in the yard. In cleaning up after dinner, Tommy's mother asked the boy to bring in her broom.

"But I'm scared to go out in the dark, Mama."

Mother answered, "The Lord is out there, honey. Don't be afraid."

So Tommy opened the back door a crack and called out, "Lord, if you're out there, hand me the broom!"

QUIET!

Six-year-old Lisa and her four-year-old brother Tim were sitting together with their parents in church, when Tim started giggling and talking out loud. "You're not supposed to talk loud in church!"

"Why? Who's going to stop me?" Tim asked.

Angie pointed to the back of the church and said, "See those two men standing by the door? They're hushers."

RED LIGHT, GREEN LIGHT

A little boy was listening to a long and tedious musical presentation by the church choir. Suddenly the red votive light by the altar caught his eye. Tugging his father's sleeve, he asked, "Daddy, when the light turns green can we go?"

HIS FIRST

Jamie was attending his first wedding. After the service, his cousin asked him, "How many women can a man marry?"

"Sixteen," was Jamie's quick answer.

"How do you know that?" his cousin asked.

"Easy," Jamie answered. "All you have

to do is add it up, like the pastor said: Four better, four worse, four richer, four poorer."

OFFERING TIME

Freddie, in church for the first time, watched as the ushers passed the offering plates. When they neared the pew where he sat, the boy piped up, "Don't pay for me, Daddy, I'm under five."

A.M. VS. P.M.

Seven-year-old Johnny had been standing in the church narthex and examining an impressively large brass plaque for some-time. Seeing the boy's interest, the pastor walked up and stood beside Johnny.
"So, what do you think of this plaque, young man?"

"What is it?" Johnny asked.

"Well, son, these are all the people who have died in the service," replied the pastor.

Soberly the child looked up at the

pastor, "Which service, sir, morning or evening?"

PRAYER REQUEST

Bobby's parents tried their best to keep him from acting up during the morning worship hour, but they were losing the battle. Finally the father picked up the little fellow and walked sternly up the aisle to apply a little discipline. Just before reaching the foyer, little Bobby called loudly to the congregation, "Pray for me! Pray for me!"

SUNDAY SCHOOL

You show me a church with a full to running over Sunday school, and I'll show you the best collection of funnies to be found anywhere. If it's not the kids making claims like "I found this dry leaf in this old Bible—think it could be Adam's underwear?" then it's the little boy who says, "The fifth commandment is 'Humor your father and your mother.'"

No, it's often the Sunday school teacher. Like the faithful soul who declares, "Not only is he the worst-behaved child in my class, but he also has perfect attendance," or the Senior Men's Bible Class teacher who asks, "What do you call a person who keeps on talking when people are no longer interested?" And a gruff voice from the corner mumbles, "A teacher."

Let's hear it for Sunday school!

Thou Shalt Not. . .

The Ten Commandments were the subject of Miss Dixie's Sunday school lesson for five and six year olds. After explaining "Honor thy father and thy mother," Miss Dixie asked, "Is there a commandment that teaches us how to treat our brothers and sisters?"

Without missing a beat, little Cindy answered, "Thou shalt not kill."

Look Up

The substitute teacher was struggling to open a lock on the Sunday school supply cabinet. She'd been told the combination but couldn't quite remember it. Finally she went to the pastor's study and asked for help.

When the minister began to twist the dial, he paused after the first couple of numbers and stared blankly. Finally he looked heavenward and his lips moved silently, then he looked back at the lock, turned to the final numbers, and clicked open the hasp.

The teacher was amazed. "I'm in awe of your faith, Pastor."

"It's really nothing," he responded. "The numbers are on a piece of tape on the ceiling."

CONTROVERSY

A ten year old, under the tutelage of a well-prepared Sunday school teacher, was becoming quite knowledgeable about the Bible. Then one day she floored her teacher when she asked, "Which virgin was the mother of Jesus, the Virgin Mary or the King James Virgin?"

HOME SWEET HOME

The teacher gathered her Sunday school group around her and exclaimed, "Well, class, all those who want to go to heaven raise your hands."

Everyone around the circle raised their hands, except one boy.

"Don't you want to go to heaven, Henry?" asked the teacher.

"I can't, ma'am," Henry replied. "My mom wants me to come straight home."

Up, Up, and Away

Miss Dixie asked her Sunday school class to draw pictures of their favorite Bible stories. She was puzzled by Larry's picture of four people on an airplane, so she asked which story he was illustrating.

"Oh, it's Mary, Joseph, and Baby Jesus on their flight to Egypt."

"But who's the fourth person, Larry?"

"Oh, that's Pontius the Pilot."

KIDS OF ISRAEL

At Twenty-third Avenue Christian Church, Charles Smith finished his Sunday school lesson. It was time for questions and answers. Up shot little Tony's hand.

"According to the Bible, Mr. Smith, the children of Israel crossed the Red Sea. Right?"

"Right."

"An' the children of Israel clobbered the Philistines, right?"

"That's right, Tony."

"An' the children of Israel built the Temple, right?"

"Right, again."

"An' the children of Israel fought the 'gyptians, an' the children of Israel fought the Romans, an' the children of Israel wuz always doin' somethin' important, right?"

"All that's right, too," agreed Smith. "So what's your question?"

"What I wanna know is this," demanded Tony. "What wuz all the grown-ups doin'?"

MEMORY VERSE

Sunday school teacher: "Do you remember your memory verse, Charlie?"

Charlie: "I sure do. I even remember the zip code. . .John 3:16."

HOW TO GET TO HEAVEN

A teacher asked the children in her Sunday school class, "If I sold my house and my car, had a big garage sale, and gave all my money to church, would I get to heaven?"

"NO!" the children all answered.

"If I cleaned the church every day, mowed the lawn, and kept everything neat and tidy, would I get to go to heaven?"

Again the answer was "NO!"

"Well," she continued, "then how can I get to heaven?"

In the back of the room, a five-year-old boy shouted, "You gotta be dead."

BELIEVE IT OR NOT

Nine-year-old Jeremy's mother asked the boy what he had learned in Sunday school.

"Well, Mom, our teacher told us how God sent Moses behind enemy lines on a rescue mission to lead the Israelites out of Egypt. When he got to the Red Sea, he and his engineers built a pontoon bridge and all the people walked across safely. Then he used his walkie-talkie to radio broadcast headquarters and call in an air strike. They sent in bombers to blow up the bridge, and all the Israelites were saved."

"Now, Jeremy, is that really what your teacher taught you?" his mother asked.

"Well, no, Mom, but if I told it the way the teacher did, you'd never believe it."

THE FATTED CALF

The primary class over at Calvary Church is taught by Tillie Shears. Last Sunday she was teaching the Prodigal Son lesson. Her aim was to emphasize the resentful attitude of the older brother.

After describing how happy the household was over the return of the wayward son, Tillie pointed out that one member of the family didn't share their joy. "Can anyone tell me who this was?"

Nine-year-old Donna Miller had been listening sympathetically to the story. She waved her hand, "I know!" she said beaming. "It was the fatted calf."

AN ORDER OF RIBS

In Miss Lilie's kindergarten Sunday school class, she was teaching how everything in the world was created by God, including human beings. Little Georgie was particularly interested in how Eve was created out of Adam's rib.

Later in the week the five-year-old's mother found him lying down as though he were ill. She asked him, "Georgie, what's the matter?"

To which Georgie replied, "I have a pain in my side. I think I'm going to have a wife."

YUMMY

Elijah and the false prophets were the subjects of Mr. Walt's Sunday school class. He explained how the true prophet built an altar and placed pieces of a sacrificial steer on it and then poured sixteen barrels of water over the whole thing. "Now," said the teacher, "can anyone tell me why the Lord asked Elijah to pour all that water over the sacrifice?"

Little Emma raised her hand with great enthusiasm and said, "To make the gravy!"

SIGN LANGUAGE

At the Sunday school picnic, Miss Smith stacked a pile of apples on one end of a table with a sign saying, "Take only one apple, please—God is watching." On the other end of the table was a pile of cookies on which a second grader had placed a sign saying, "Take all the cookies you want—God is watching the apples."

OUT OF THE MOUTHS OF KIDS

After graphically telling the story of the Good Samaritan, in which a man was brutally beaten, robbed, and left for dead, Mrs. Martin asked her Sunday school class, "If you saw a person lying beside the road all wounded and bleeding, what would you do?"

A thoughtful little Maggie broke the hushed silence, "I think I'd throw up."

MORE Q'S & A'S

Teacher: "Why do we say 'Amen' at the end of a prayer instead of 'Awomen'?"

Smartie: "The same reason we sing
'Hymns' instead of 'Hers'!"

Teacher: "What do you call a sleep-
walking nun?"
Smartie: "A roamin' Catholic."

Teacher: "Why didn't Noah go fishing?"
Smartie: "He only had two worms."

Teacher: "When was the longest day in
the Bible?"
Smartie: "The day Adam was created,
because there was no Eve."

QUICKIES

Sunday School Teacher: "What must
you do to
receive the
forgiveness
of sin?"
Teddy: "Sin."

Sunday School Teacher: "Now, who decreed that all the world should be taxed?"

Carla: "The Democrats."

Teddy: "Who was Round John Virgin?"

Carla: "One of the Twelve Opossums."

Sunday School Teacher: "What are the sins of omission?"

Teddy: "They're ones we ought to have committed but haven't."

Teddy: "Is it true that shepherds have dirty socks?"

Carla: "What do you mean?"

Teddy: ."I heard the
                          shepherds
                          washed their
                          socks by night."

WHAT I LEARNED IN SUNDAY SCHOOL

The Egyptians were all drowned in the dessert.

Afterwards, Moses went up on Mount Cyanide to get the ten amendments.

Moses died before he ever reached Canada.

Solomon, one of David's sons, had three hundred wives and seven hundred porcupines.

Jesus was born because Mary had an immaculate contraption.

Jesus enunciated the Golden Rule, which says to do one to others before they do one to you.

St. Paul cavorted to Christianity. He preached holy acrimony, which is another name for marriage.

DEAR SUNDAY SCHOOL TEACHER. . .

"Please say a prayer for our Little League team. We need God's help or a new pitcher. Thank you." Alexander, age ten

"I know God loves everybody, but He never met my sister." Arnold, age eight

LET THERE BE ANIMALS

Every parent-type reading this has had to man- or woman-up to the eternal question, "Will Fido go to heaven?" As far as we know, no one has created a Four Spiritual Laws tract for God's creatures. On St. Francis Sunday, some churches have a blessing of the animals. But according to most theologies, count on enjoying your four-footed brethren in the here and now. Of course, God did have a sense of humor when he said, "Let there be aardvarks."

A DOG TALE

Margaret and Fred Ziggler wanted a "truly Christian" dog. So they went to a kennel that specialized in that particular breed. There they found a dog they liked. When they asked him to fetch a Bible, he did it in a flash. When they instructed him to look up John 3:16, he turned right to it. "Oh, we'll take this pup, he's wonderful," said Margaret and Fred.

That night the Zigglers invited friends from their church over to meet the remarkable dog. The guests were impressed with Fido's ability to do Christian tricks, "Can he do regular dog tricks, too?" they asked. That stopped the Zigglers cold; they'd never even thought of that.

"Well," they said, "let's try this out." So they clearly pronounced the command, "Heel!"

Quick as a wink, the dog jumped up, put his paw on Ziggler's forehead, closed his eyes in concentration, and bowed his head.

TALE OF A CAT

| Sunday School Teacher: | "Why would it be wrong to cut off a cat's tail?" |
| Prissy: | "The Bible says, 'What God has put together, let no man put asunder.'" |

"I'M NOT LION"

This story was told for true at a recent missions conference. . .but don't you believe it!

A stalwart young missionary was chased through the African bush for a week by a ferocious lion. Finally the missionary found himself cornered and, in despair, fell to his knees and prayed for deliverance. To his amazement, the lion also began to pray.

"It's truly a miracle," said the missionary, "you, a killer lion, joining me in prayer just when I thought my life was going to end!"

"Be quiet," said the lion, "I'm saying grace."

NOAH IT ALL

Noah's remark as the animals boarded the ark, "Now I've herd everything."

A LIMERICK

Ferrets live by a code tried and true,
From which humans can benefit, too:
Teach your sons and your daughters
To do unto otters
As otters would do unto you.

GO FORTH AND MULTIPLY

After the flood water went down and
Noah lowered the ramp, he told the animals to go forth and multiply.

All the animals left except two snakes
who lay quietly in the corner of the ark.
"Why don't you go forth and multiply?"
asked Noah.

"We can't," answered the snakes.
"We're adders."

NOT LEARNED AT CHURCH

A cat and a mouse died on the same day
and went up to heaven. While strolling

down the golden street they met God, and He asked them, "How do you like it so far?"

The mouse replied, "It's great, but can I have a pair of in-line skates?"

God said, "Sure," and He gave the mouse the skates.

Next day God saw the cat and asked him, "How do you like it up here so far?"

The cat replied, "Great, I didn't know you had Meals on Wheels."

HE'S A BEAR, ISN'T HE?

The class was all excited. The kids had a riddle to stump their Sunday school teacher:

Q: What do Winnie the Pooh and John the Baptist have in common?

A: They both have the same middle name.

MISSIONARY HORSE

Lost and hungry in the desert for a week, an American tourist finally spies a little church on the edge of the wilderness. Tired and weak, he collapses on the front porch, where a missionary finds him and cares for him. When the tourist is rested and ready to go on his way, he asks directions to the nearest town.

"Would you like to borrow my horse?" the missionary asks.

The American responds, "Yes!"

"Well, there is something special about this horse. You must say 'Thank God' to make him go and 'Amen' to make him stop."

Not paying much attention the tourist says, "Sure, okay."

So the tourist mounts the animal and says, "Thank God," and the horse starts walking. Then he says "Thank God, thank God," and the horse starts trotting. Finally feeling brave, the man says, "Thank God, thank God, thank God," and the horse leaps into a full gallop.

Suddenly a bluff with a three hundred foot drop appears on the horizon, and he does everything he can to make the horse stop. "Whoa! Stop! Help! Whoa!" Finally he remembers, "Amen!" and the horse stops four inches from the drop-off. Exhausted, the tourist leans back in his saddle and breathes a prayer, "Thank God!"

A GOLDEN OLDIE

Little John was bothered with a question that he had to ask his Sunday school teacher. "Miss Davis, are there any animals in heaven?"

"I'm not sure, Johnny," his teacher responded.

"Well, I just wanted to know, 'cause last Sunday we sang about "Gladly the Cross-Eyed Bear."

TRAINED DOG

A minister preached a very short sermon. He explained, "My dog got into my study and chewed up some of my notes."

At the close of the service a visitor asked, "If your dog ever has pups, please let my pastor have one of them."

OH, OH

Charles: "How did you know I was the one who put the tadpoles in the punch at the Sunday school picnic?"

Teacher: "A little bird told me."

Charles: "Well, it must have been a stool pigeon."

BUT I'M A PASTOR. . .

"Hello, Pastor Martin? I've lost my cat and. . ."

"Sorry, I really don't think that I can

look for your cat right now."

"But don't you understand. . .this is a very intelligent cat. He's almost human. He can practically talk."

"Well, maybe you'd better hang up, sister; he may be trying to phone you right now."

CLUCK, CLUCK

Final exam in Mr. Smith's Sunday school class.

Q: Which came first, the chicken or the egg?

A: The chicken, of course. God couldn't lay an egg.

HEADS AND TAILS

Young Reverend Smith was a bachelor and staunch sportsman. He was the epitome of the great white hunter. On his parsonage walls hung trophies of his animal kills.

Millie Jones was being courted by

Smith. The first time she visited her boyfriend's parsonage home, she came face to face with the mounted animal heads. "Why do you have those heads on your walls?" she asked.

"Because they are such beautiful animals," was his reply.

"Well," reasoned Millie, "I think my mother is attractive, but I have photographs of her."

DEACONS, BISHOPS, AND OTHER BRASS

Every organization has its top dogs, the brass, the guys who were kicked upstairs and who keep an eye on their ligament or limb in the Body of Christ. Some churches carry their top leader around on their shoulders, others wear medieval chapeaus and carry gold shepherd's crooks, still others carry their exalted office in less showy ways—in black Armani suits.

In actuality, it's the local church leadership that bears the brunt of most church humor—boards and vestries, deacons and committee chairs, head ushers and sextons (don't get excited, that's Episcopal jargon for janitor). Fasten your seat belts, this is going to be a bumpy ride!

PASTOR: GOOD NEWS/BAD NEWS

Good: Your biggest critic just left your church.

Bad: He has been appointed Head Bishop in your denomination.

Good: Your deacons want to send you to the Holy Land.

Bad: They are stalling until the next war.

Good: The trustees finally voted to add more church parking.

Bad: They are going to blacktop the front lawn of your parsonage.

Good: The Elder Board accepted your job description the way you wrote it.

Bad: They were so inspired by it, they formed a search committee to find someone capable of filling the position.

Good: You finally found a choir director who matches your way of doing things exactly.

Bad: The choir mutinied.

Good: The youth in your church come to
      your house for a surprise visit.
Bad: It's in the middle of the night, and
      they are armed with toilet paper
      and shaving cream to decorate
      your house.

Good: Your women's softball team finally
      won a game.
Bad: They beat your men's team.

THE CHURCH BOARD

"There will be a meeting of the board
immediately following this service,"
announced the pastor. After the benediction the group gathered for the called
meeting. All looked askance when a visitor
who had never attended their church
before joined them.

    "My friend," asked the pastor, "did you
understand that this a meeting of the

board? "Yes," said the visitor, "and after that service, I'm about as bored as you can get!"

MULE

Pastor: "Say, Deacon, a mule died out in front of the church."

Deacon: "Well, it's the job of you ministers to look after the dead. Why tell me?"

Pastor: "You're right; it is my job. But we always notify the next of kin."

FORGIVENESS?

Old Jack and old John had been board members at Prince of Peace Lutheran for as long as anyone could remember. They were constantly at odds with each other and at each other's throats, especially in church board meetings. When one would vote "yes," the other would have to vote "no."

One day old Jack died and arrived at Heaven's gates. He noticed how everyone was asked a question before they proceeded in. When it was his turn, St. Peter said, "Hi, Jack. To see if you qualify to come in, I have to ask you to spell "Jesus.""

"That's easy," said Jack, and so he spelled, "J-E-S-U-S." Peter complimented Jack and then asked if he would do him a small favor, "Just take over here for a few minutes."

Several people were waiting at the gate, and Jack asked each one the same question, "Will you please spell 'Jesus'?" Then Jack could hardly believe his eyes; old John was in line.

"What are you doing here?" John asked.

"I'm just filling in for St. Peter. I'm asking everyone to spell a word before they can go through the gates."

"Oh, yeah?" John exclaimed. "What's the word?"

After thinking a moment, Jack said, "Spell 'Albuquerque.'"

Haircut Homily

A small town's only barber was known for his arrogant and negative attitude. When one of his customers mentioned he'd be going to Rome on a vacation and hoped to meet the pope, the barber's reaction was typical. "You?" he said. "Meet the pope? Don't make me laugh! The pope sees kings and presidents. What would he want with you?"

A month later, the man returned for another haircut. "How was Rome?" asked the barber.

"Great! I saw the pope!"

"On his balcony from St. Peter's Square? With the rest of the crowds?"

"Yes, but then two of his Swiss Guards came up and said the pope wanted to meet me and took me right into his private apartment in the Vatican."

"Really?" the barber asked. "What did he say?"

"He said, 'Who gave you that lousy haircut?'"

SACRED SECRETS

And did you hear the one about the bishop who hired a secretary who had worked for the Pentagon? She immediately changed his filing system to "Sacred" and "Top Sacred."

THE BISHOP'S VISIT

Little Johnny's dad was the pastor of a small church in the Midwest. One day, he told Johnny that a very important church leader, a bishop, was coming to the church and would be staying with them in their home. Little Johnny became very excited about meeting the bishop. "What do I get to do?" he asked.

"Your job," father answered, "will be to take his morning tea up to the guest room."

"What shall I say?" little Johnny asked.

"Just remember to say, 'It's the boy, my Lord, it's time to get up.'"

Little Johnny was very excited. He rehearsed his lines, repeating them over and over. Finally the day came, and little Johnny had learned all his lines. At the appointed hour, the bishop's tea and a biscuit were set on a tray and given to little Johnny to take to the guest. Knocking on the visitor's door, the boy become so excited his lines got all mixed up, so when he finally spoke, out came, "It's the Lord, my boy, and your time is up."

Missing Deacon

Deacon Roberts was leaving the morning service on Sunday morning. At the door, the pastor reached out and shook Robert's hand. "By the way, Deacon, you need to join the army of the Lord."

"I'm already in the army of the Lord, Pastor."

"Then why do I see you only at Christmas and Easter?"

Deacon Roberts whispered back, "I'm in the secret service."

A Deacon Tells Him

There was an energetic young preacher who took his sermonizing very seriously. Now there was a deacon in his congregation who did very little and seemed to care less. The preacher often took aim at the deacon in his preaching, but the old deacon never caught the point. He always thought pastor was preaching to someone else.

One Sunday the preacher was particularly pointed. Following the service, the deacon exclaimed, "Preacher, you sure told 'em today."

The next sermon, it was the same reaction again.

The third Sunday, the preacher was even more pointed. Again the deacon enthused, "Preacher, you sure told 'em today."

The fourth Sunday it rained so hard that no one came to church except the pastor and his deacon. Preacher thought he'd now have a real opportunity to take aim and hit his deacon-target. After a hard hitting thirty minutes and a hymn of invitation, the pastor went to his place at the door to greet his one-person congregation.

In a moment the deacon walked up to his pastor, held out his hand, and announced, "Preacher, you'd sure told 'em if they had been here!"

DON'T BLAME ME

A new pastor visited a children's Sunday school department. After standing quietly at the back for a few minutes, he asked the youngsters, "Who tore down the walls of Jericho?"

"It wasn't me," shouted young Tommy.

The pastor was unfazed and repeated, "Come on now, who tore down the walls of Jericho?"

The teacher took the pastor to one side. "Look, Pastor, Tommy's a good boy. If he said he didn't do it, he didn't do it. I believe him."

The pastor couldn't comprehend what

he was hearing, and later that day he related the story to the Director of Christian Ed. The director frowned. "I know we have had trouble with Tommy in the past. I'll have a word with him."

By now totally baffled, the pastor left and approached the deacon. Once again he told the whole story, including the responses of the teacher and the Christian Ed director.

The deacon listened patiently and smiled, "Yes, Pastor, I can see your problem. But I suggest we take the money from the general fund to pay for the walls and leave it at that."

PASTOR HANGING

The chairman of the Pastor Search Committee informed the congregation, "Next Sunday our 'try-out' preacher will be the Reverend Bill Johnson. If you would like to see the other preachers, you will find them hanging in the vestibule."

A Pious Man

Charlie Jones was a pious man who had been head usher at Central Church for seventy-five years. On his one hundred-fifth birthday he stopped going to church. Alarmed by the old fellow's absence after so many years of faithful service, Pastor Anderson went to see him.

He found Charlie in excellent health, so the minister asked, "How come after all these years we don't see you any more?"

The old man looked around and lowered his voice, "I'll tell you, Pastor," he whispered, "when I got to be ninety, I expected God to take me home any day. But then when I got to be ninety-five, then one hundred, then 105. So I figured that God is very busy and must've forgotten about me—and I don't want to remind Him."

Search Committee Report

The following is a confidential report on

several candidates being considered for a ministry position.

Adam:	Good man but has problems with his wife. Also, one reference to how he and his wife enjoy skinny dipping.
Noah:	Prone to unrealistic building projects.
Abraham:	There are rumors about his strange relationship to his wife.
Joseph:	A big thinker, but a bit of a braggart. Believes in dream interpreting, has a prison record, and has been accused of adultery.
Moses:	A modest and meek man, but a poor communicator—even stutters at times. Sometimes blows his stack and acts rashly.
David:	The most promising candidate of all until we discovered his affair with his

neighbor's wife. His kids are out of control. Worse yet, he's a proponent of upbeat musical expressions.

Solomon: Great preacher, but our parsonage would never hold all those wives. Good with building projects, but rather extravagant.

Samson: Hair too long.

Elijah: Prone to depression. Spends too much time by himself— a loner. No wife that we know of.

Methuselah: Too old. Way too old.

Jonah: Ran away from God's call. Known to pout when things don't go his way. Tells questionable fish stories.

John: Says he's a Baptist, but definitely doesn't dress like one. Has a weird diet. Offends politicians and is known to lose his head.

Jesus: Seldom stays in one place

very long. He's single.
Some say he has a Messiah
complex.

Peter: Too blue collar. Has a bad
temper. Has even been
known to curse. Claims to
have visions.

Paul: Powerful CEO-type leader
and fascinating preacher.
Considered short on tact,
unforgiving with younger
ministers, seemingly harsh,
and has been known to
preach all night. Controver-
sial on women's issues. Little
chance that he'll ever marry.

Timothy: Too young.

Judas: His references are solid. A
steady plodder. Conservative
and pragmatic. Good con-
nections. Knows how to
handle money. We're inviting
him to preach next Sunday.
Possibilities here.

BREAKING THE SILENCE

The Monastery of Silence was led by an ancient Abbott, who took the brothers' vow of silence very seriously. When Brother John entered the monastery and took his silence vow, the Abbot reminded him, "You are welcome here as long as you like, but you may not speak until I direct you to do so."

Brother John lived in the monastery for a full year before the Abbot said to him, "Brother John, you have been here a year now, you may speak two words."

Brother John said, "Hard bed." So the Abbot got him a better bed.

The next year, Brother John was called by the Abbott. "You may say another two words, Brother John."

"Cold food," announced Brother John, so the Abbott promised the food would improve.

On his third anniversary at the monastery, the Abbott again called Brother John into his office. "You may say two more words today."

"I quit," announced Brother John.

"It is probably for the best," said the Abbott. "All you have done since you got here is complain."

Now I Believe!

Pastor Jackson used this story to illustrate the point of belief in his Sunday morning homily.

An atheist was spending a quiet day fishing when suddenly his boat was attacked by the Loch Ness monster. In one graceful flip, the legendary beast tossed the atheist high into the air. Then it opened its mouth to swallow both the man and the boat. As the man sailed head over heels, he cried out, "Oh, my God! Help me!"

Immediately, the ferocious attack scene froze, leaving the atheist hanging in midair. Then a booming voice came out of the clouds. "I thought you didn't believe in me!"

"Come on, God, give me a break," the man pleaded. "Two minutes ago I didn't believe in the Loch Ness monster, either!"

THE PARSONAGE FAMILY

The folks who live under the roof of any church parsonage or vicarage or manse or whatever you call it, should be exempt from jokes and snappy sayings. But who is more vulnerable? Consider the pastor's wife, "Far above rubies" says the writer of Ecclesiastes. "More like a chipped zircon," admits the honest "parsonette" at Central Methodist.

And then there are the parsonage children. The youth group holds its collective breath and keep their fingers crossed until the guys view the new minister's daughters and the girls behold the sons.

Talk about a goldfish bowl. . .

HOORAY!

A minister from the city was filling the pulpit in a small community. After the service he was invited over to the house of one of the members for lunch.

In the course of the conversation, he talked about his family back home, and how his son won first place in the one-hundred-yard dash.

"I know just how you must feel," declared the man of the house. "I remember how pleased I was last year when our pig got the blue ribbon at the fair."

SECOND TIME AROUND

The minister's wife was a wonder at conserving food and rarely had to throw away a bit of it. At one meal she served her pastor husband nothing but leftovers that the parson viewed with great disdain. He began to pick at the food, causing his wife to say, "Dear, you forgot the blessing."

"Listen, sweetheart, if you can show me one item that hasn't been blessed at least two times, I can't see what another prayer can do for it."

A TV Crowd

The pastor of First Church preached to his congregation about the bad influence television had on Christians. He exhorted everyone to do what he did in his own home. "I believe everyone in this church should put their TV sets in the closet and leave them there."

Just then his wife turned around and said to the friend behind her, "Yes, but it's getting pretty crowded in there."

No Kiddin'

Pastor Father: "I never kissed a girl before I married your mother. Will you be able to tell your children that?"

Parsonage Son: "Not with a straight face."

FACT FINDING

The average American parsonage family consists of 4.1 persons. You have one guess as to who constitutes the .1 person.

Pastor Husband: "I think there is insanity in my family. They keep asking me for money."

Parsonage brother to his sister:
"Sis, it isn't good manners to eat chicken with your fingers. You should eat your fingers separately."

Pastor Husband: "What have you been doing with all the grocery money I gave you?"

Wife: "Turn sideways and look in the mirror."

Parsonage Daughter: "I'm sorry, but I don't kiss on the first date."

Boy: "How about on the last one?"

LESSON IN FINANCE

Reverend Martin, settled in his parsonage study, sorts through the mail and comes upon an envelope from the bank. "Well, the bank returned the last check you wrote."

To which his wife replies, "Oh, good. What shall we buy with it this time?"

LAP TOP

Mrs. Reverend George Martin wanted to surprise her husband with a computer for his birthday. When the salesman suggested a laptop, Mrs. Martin burst into laughter. "What's so funny about that?" the salesman asked.

"Sir, my husband hasn't had a lap for twenty years."

NO DISRESPECT IMPLIED

Pastor Smith had a long session in his dentist's chair having all of his teeth pulled and a set of dentures installed and was back in his pulpit the following Lord's Day.

The first Sunday he preached only ten minutes.

The second Sunday he preached twenty minutes.

But on the third Sunday he preached for an hour and a half.

When some members asked about the time variations, he responded: "The first Sunday, my gums were so sore it hurt to talk. The second Sunday, my dentures were hurting a lot. The third Sunday, I accidentally grabbed my wife's dentures—and I couldn't stop talking!"

DAD'S JOB

Three boys are in the church yard bragging about their fathers. The first boy declares, "My Dad scribbles a few words on a piece of paper; he calls it a poem, and they give him fifty dollars."

The second boy says, "That's nothing, my Dad scribbles a few words on a piece of paper; he calls it a song, and they give him one hundred dollars."

Little Johnny says, "I got you both beat. My Dad scribbles a few words on a piece of paper; he calls it a sermon, and it takes eight people to carry all the money!"

Pastoral Visit

The minister's little daughter was sent to bed with a stomachache and missed her usual romp with her daddy. A few minutes later she appeared at the top of the stairs and called to he mother, "Mama, let me talk with Daddy."

"No, my dear, not tonight. He's at board meeting. Get back to bed."

"Please, Mama."

"I said no. That's enough now."

"Mother, I'm a very sick woman, and I must see my pastor at once."

PUNISHMENT

Parsonage Son: "Dad, you wouldn't punish me for something I didn't do, would you?"

Pastor Dad: "Why, of course not."

Parsonage Son: "Good! I didn't do my homework."

Pastor Dad: "Well, son, remember I'm spanking you because I love you."

Parsonage Son: "I sure wish I was big enough to return your love."

THE EASTER DRESS

The poor country parson was livid when he confronted his wife with the receipt for a $250 dress she had bought. "How could you do this!" he exclaimed.

"I don't know," she wailed, "I was standing in the store looking at the dress. Then I found myself trying it on. It was like the devil was whispering to me, 'Wow, you look great in that dress. You should buy it.' "

"Well," the husband persisted, "you know how to deal with the tempter. Just tell him, 'Get behind me, Satan!' "

"I did," replied his wife, "but then he said, 'It looks great from back there, too!' "

World Ruler

Pastor George and wife Sally brought their new bundle of joy home to the parsonage. Days went by with Sally watching every move baby Georgie made while George Sr. busied himself with heavy global and theological thoughts. Naturally the care began to take its toll on Sally, causing her husband to gallantly announce:

George: "I know you're having a lot of trouble with Georgie, dear, but keep in mind, 'the hand that rocks the cradle is the hand that rules the world.' "

Sally: "How about taking over the world for a few hours while I go shopping?"

MESS

Parsonage son to his mother: "I've decided that I want to be a preacher so that I can clean up the mess the world is in."

"That's just wonderful," purred his mother. "You can go upstairs and start with your room."

SHOCKER

Mr. Johnson, a businessman from Wisconsin, went on a business trip to Louisiana. He immediately sent an E-mail back to his wife Jean. Unfortunately, he mistyped a letter and the E-mail ended up going to a Mrs. Joan Johnson, the wife of a preacher who just passed away.

The preacher's widow took one look at the E-mail and promptly fainted. When she was revived, she nervously pointed to the message, which read, "Arrived safely, but it sure is hot down here!"

More Visitation

Pastor Jackson habitually told his congregation that if they needed a pastoral visit to drop a note in the offering plate. One evening after service he discovered a note that read: "I am one of your loneliest members and heaviest contributors. May I have a visit tomorrow evening?" It was signed, "Your wife."

Family Worship

Every evening the Reverend Phillips family gathered together for a Bible story and prayer. One evening, the story was about Lot and his wife escaping from Sodom and Gomorrah. As all know, the great climax of the narrative is when Mrs. Lot looks back and turns into a pillar of salt.

The story sat well with Tommy, who raised his hand the second the story was over and told his father, "That's like when mom was driving home in the car; she looked back at Rachel and me and turned into a telephone pole."

THE GOOD BOOK

Human misunderstanding is often the basis for humor about the Bible. It's not that anyone is laughing at the Bible; it's more like we're laughing at our misunderstanding of the Bible. Or maybe it's one of those nervous titters that reveal how much we do know. Mark Twain hit the nail on the head with this observation: "Most people are bothered by those passages of Scripture they do not understand, but the passages that bother me are those I do understand."

HANDLE WITH CARE

There was this well-meaning lady mailing a box of Bibles for her church to missionaries overseas. "Is there anything breakable in here?" asked the postal clerk.

"Only the Ten Commandments," answered the lady.

A MISUNDERSTANDING

Two church attenders had just come from church and a sermon on Sodom and Gomorrah from Genesis. "You know, George, I always thought that Sodom and Gomorrah were man and wife."

His friend replied, "I can believe you, because I thought the Epistles were the wives of the Apostles."

GARDEN OF EATIN'

One of the Community Church pastor's favorite premarital counseling jokes is this one: Adam and Eve had an ideal marriage. He didn't have to hear about all the men she could have married, and she didn't have to hear about the way his mother cooked.

More Adam and Eve

The story of Adam and Eve was being carefully explained in the primary Vacation Bible School class. Following the story, the children were asked to draw a picture to illustrate some part of the story.

Little Emily was most interested and drew a picture of a car with three people in it. In the front seat behind the wheel was a rather large man and in the back seat a man and a woman.

The teacher was at a loss to understand how this illustrated the lesson. But little Emily was prompt with her explanation. "Why, this is God driving Adam and Eve out of the garden."

Good Night

God: "Whew! I just created a twenty-four-hour period of alternating light and darkness on earth."

Angel: "What are you going to do now?"

God: "Call it a day."

THE BIBLE IN FIFTY WORDS

God made
Adam bit
Noah arked
Abraham split
Jacob fooled
Joseph ruled
Bush talked
Moses balked
Pharaoh plagued
People walked
Sea divided
Tablets guided
Promise landed
Saul freaked
David peeked
Prophets warned
Jesus born
God walked
Love talked
Anger crucified
Hope died
Love rose
Spirit flamed
Word spread
God remained

LOT

A father was reading a Bible story to his young son. He read, "The man named Lot was warned to take his wife and flee out of the city, but his wife looked back and was turned into a pillar of salt."

His son asked, "What happened to the flea?"

PLAYING ON SUNDAY

George's wife was worried about her husband playing ball on Sunday. She searched through the Bible for direction but could find nothing. Finally she went to her pastor. "Is it a sin for George to play ball on Sunday?"

To which the minister retorted, "It's not a sin, but the way he plays, it's a crime."

TURN ABOUT

A preacher who suffered extreme strained relations with his congregation was finally appointed chaplain at the state prison. Elated to be rid of him so easily, the people came in great numbers to hear his farewell sermon. The preacher chose as his text John 14:3, "I go and prepare a place for you. . .that where I am, there ye may be also."

WHICH VERSION?

Jesus said unto his disciples, "Whom do men say that I am?"

And his disciples answered unto Him, "Master, Thou art the supreme eschatological manifestation of omnipotent ecclesiastical authority, the absolute, divine, sacerdotal monarch."

And Jesus said, "What!?"

TEN COMMANDMENTS

Merrie's Bible school teacher asked her to list the Ten Commandments in any order. Her answer? "Six, three, five, four, eight, seven, ten, one, nine, two."

DRAWING GOD

A children's Sunday school teacher encouraged her five year olds to create an art masterpiece that related to the Bible. As she wandered around the room looking at the pictures, she came to little Alice. "Alice, what are you drawing?"

"I'm drawing God."

"But no one knows what God looks like, Alice."

Without missing a beat, Alice replied, "They will when I'm finished."

CONTENTS

Minister:	"Do you know what's in the Bible?"
Little Girl:	"Yes, I think I know every thing that's in it."
Minister:	"You do? Tell me."
Little Girl:	"Okay. There's a picture of my brother's girlfriend, a ticket stub, a picture of my schnauzer, and a secret note from Terry."

ANOTHER Q & A

Miss Spencer: "Tim, what evidence is
there in the Bible that
Adam and Eve were noisy?"

Tim: "They raised Cain."

LEFTOVERS

A nervous preacher forgot his notes for the
sermon he was about to deliver. So he decided to "wing" it. In the middle of his address
he got a few things twisted when he
declared that the Lord took four thousand
barley loaves and six thousand fishes and fed
twenty-four people, and had plenty left over.

A heckler in the congregation called
out, "Anybody could do that, preacher."

"Could you?" asked the minister.

"Certainly I could."

After the service when the preacher
complained about the interrupter's conduct, he was told of his error by a deacon.

"Well, next week I will not forget my
notes. I'll fix that character."

The next week the minister stepped forward confidently and began his sermon. In the course of his remarks, he corrected the numbers mentioned last Sunday. He told how five barley loaves and two fishes had fed the multitude of probably twenty-four thousand people. Then he pointed to the previous Sunday's heckler and asked, "Could you do that?"

"I sure could," said the heckler.

"And just how would you do it?" asked the preacher.

"With the loaves and fishes left over from last Sunday."

PARABLE IN "F"

When Josh Skiles was in seminary, his homiletics professor told the preaching class how important it is to use alliteration in one's sermon. Josh took it to heart, so on his first Sunday behind a pulpit, he presented this alliterated sermon based on The Prodigal Son story:

Feeling footloose and frisky, a feather-
    brained fellow
Forced his fond father to fork over the
    farthings
And flew far to foreign fields
And fabulously frittered his fortune with
    faithless friends.
Fleeced by his fellows in folly and facing
    famine,
He found himself a feed-flinger in a filthy
    farmyard.
Fairly famishing, he fain would've filled
    his frame
With foraged food from fodder fragments.
"Fooey, my father's flunkies fare far finer,"
The frazzled fugitive forlornly fumbled,
    frankly facing facts.
Frustrated by failure and filled with
    foreboding,
He fled forthwith to his family.
Falling at his father's feet, he forlornly
    fumbled, "Father, I've flunked,
And fruitlessly forfeited family fellowship
    and favor."

The farsighted father, forestalling further
    flinching,
Frantically flagged their flunkies.
"Fetch a fatling from the flock and fix
    a feast."
The fugitive's faultfinding brother
    frowned
On fickle forgiveness of former folderol.
But the faithful father figured,
"Filial fidelity is fine, but the fugitive is
    found!
What forbids fervent festivity?
Let flags be unfurled! Let fanfares flare!"
Father's forgiveness formed the foundation
For the former fugitive's future fortitude!

PREACHINGS AND TEACHINGS AND STUFF

Sometime when you have nothing better to do, peruse the Saturday newspaper church page and check on Sunday sermon topics, lessons, announcements, guest speakers, out-of-town musicians, and hints for living the good life. Note the head-shots of your community clerics. Pay attention to the ones where the minister husband and his wife pose together in the photo; those are usually indications that both think their faces and hairdos will contribute to outreach evangelism.

The humor in all of this is in how complicated the communication of faith has become. Wasn't it Thomas Jefferson who said, "It is in our lives, and not in our words, that our religion must be read"? That was before telephone and television evangelism, bus and puppet ministries, and celebrity endorsements. So what difference does it make that your

pastor and wife are the Ken and Barbie of
the Saturday church page?

WHY SERMONS?

An anonymous letter writer sent his/her
letter to the local newspaper editor complaining that church attendance made no
sense. "I've gone for thirty years," he wrote,
"and have heard something like three
thousand sermons. But for the life of me,
I can't remember a single one of them. So
I think I'm wasting my time, as are the
preachers for even bothering to deliver a
sermon at all."

This letter started a real controversy on
the op-ed page. It went on for weeks until
someone wrote this clincher:

"I've been married for thirty years. In
that time my wife has cooked some thirty-
two thousand meals, but for the life of me,
I can recall the menu of few if any of those
meals. I do know, though, they all nour-
ished me and gave me the strength I need

to do my work. If my wife had not given me those meals, I'd be dead today."

No more comments about sermon contents have appeared on the op-ed page.

HEAR SAY

Pastor: "How did the assistant pastor's sermon go Sunday?"

Member: "It was a poor sermon. Nothing in it at all."

(Upon seeing the assistant pastor)

Pastor: "How did it go Sunday morning?"

Assistant: "Excellently. I didn't have time to prepare anything myself, so I preached one of yours."

FUNNY, ISN'T IT?

Funny how tiring it is to serve God for one hour, but how quickly a team plays sixty minutes of basketball.

Funny how long a couple of hours spent at church are, but how short they are when watching a movie.

Funny how we can't think of anything to say when we pray, but how easy it is to chat with a friend.

Funny how thrilled we get when a baseball game goes extra innings, but we complain when a sermon is longer than usual.

Funny how we want a front seat at a game or concert but scramble to get a back seat at church.

Funny how we need a two- or three-week notice to fit a church event into our schedule, but can adjust our schedule at the last minute for other events.

Funny how big one hundred dollars looks when you take it to church, but it's so small at the mall.

Funny how hard it is to read a chapter in the Bible, but how easy it is to read one hundred pages of a best-seller.

Funny how hard it is for people to learn a simple plan of salvation, but how simple it is for the same people to understand and repeat gossip.

Funny how we believe what the newspaper says, but question what the Bible says.

WATER BAPTISM

A drought in Georgia began to affect how the churches in many communities had to conduct baptisms. The Baptists took up sprinkling, the Methodists used damp cloths, and the Presbyterians gave out rain checks.

A NO-NO

"When you take sermon material from one writer, it's plagiarism; but when you swipe it from many writers, it's research."

MAJORS AND MINORS

A preacher spoke twenty minutes on Isaiah, twenty minutes on Ezekiel, twenty minutes on Jeremiah, and twenty minutes on Daniel. Then he announced, "We have now come to the twelve minor prophets. What place will I give Hosea?"

A man on the back row shouted out, "I'm leaving. Give Hosea my place."

SEZ MARK TWAIN

The great American writer Mark Twain told the story about his session in church one Sunday morning. It seems the preacher was very good and the sermon quite wonderful. About halfway through, Twain decided to give twenty dollars to the church. But the preacher went on and on until the novelist thought to cut his contribution in half. On and on went the preacher until Twain decided that when the basket was passed he'd give only two dollars. Finally, at long last, the sermon ended; when the basket came his way, the great Mark Twain filched a dollar out of it.

PREMARITAL COUNSELING

All Saints Church's Fr. John Nixon's best advice to those soon-to-be-wed: "Keep your eyes wide open before marriage—half shut afterwards."

"Marriage is like a violin—after the music stops, the strings are still attached."

"The most dangerous year in married life is the first, followed by the second, third, fourth, fifth. . ."

THAT IS THE QUESTION

A preacher once asked an actor why he had such large audiences and he, the preacher, had only a small audience at church.

"I act as if I believe in what I say," said the actor, "while you preach as if you did not believe what you're saying."

An Observation

First Preacher: "I think a pastor needs to study diligently for his Sunday morning message."

Second Preacher: "I disagree. Many times I have no idea what I am going to preach about, but I go into the pulpit and preach and think nothing of it."

First Preacher: "And you are quite right in thinking nothing of it. Your deacons have told me they share your opinion."

Church Nursery Sign

1 Corinthians 15:51: "We shall not all sleep, but we shall be changed."

NARTHEX SIGN

A little girl sitting in church with her father suddenly felt ill. "Daddy," she whispered, "I have to frow up!" Her father told her to hurry to the rest room.

In less than that two minutes the child was back. "I didn't have to go too far," she explained. "There's a box by the front door with a sign that says, 'For the sick.'"

SLIP OF THE TONGUE

A just-out-of-seminary pastor was about to conduct his first wedding and was worried sick. An elderly preacher gave him some advice, "If you lose your place in the ceremony book or you forget your lines, start quoting scriptures until you find your place."

The wedding day came. And, sure enough, the young man forgot where he was in the ritual. Unfortunately, the only verse he could think of was, "Father, forgive them, for they know not what they do."

AN AWFUL TRUTH

Absence makes the heart grow fonder. If that is so, a huge bunch of people sure love their church.

REAL SECURITY

Caruthersville is such a small town that it only has one church and no barbershop. So to stem the tide, Baptist preacher Harley pastors the little church and during the week becomes the town barber.

Well, in Caruthersville lived a successful man who decided that he wanted to show off his wealth by getting a daily shave at Pastor Harley's barbershop.

Now, when the preacher had to go out visit the sick and shut-ins, his wife Grace picked up the shears and razoring responsibilities. As a matter of fact, it just so happened that Grace was holding forth when the successful man came in for his first shave and shave him she did. "How much do I owe you?" he asked Grace.

"That'll be twenty-five dollars." Even though it seemed a bit steep, the man paid up and left the shop feeling very successful.

The next morning he woke up and rubbed his chin. Why, his face was as smooth as it was the day before. The same thing happened the following morning and the next, too. Perplexed, the successful man went back to the barber shop and asked how he kept his clean-shaven look.

This particular day Pastor Harley was in, and his answer to the successful man's question was, "Friend, you were shaved by Grace—and once shaved, always shaved."

THE MESSAGE BOARD

In an effort to provide a silent sermon to the neighborhood, First United Methodist erected a message board on the front lawn. As a result of a congregational contest, the following (unoriginal) messages were selected.

"Free trip to heaven. Details inside."

"Try our Sundays. They are better than Baskin-Robbins."

"Searching for a new look? Have your faith lifted here!"

"People are like tea bags—you have to put them in hot water before you know how strong they are."

"Running low on faith? Stop in for a fill-up."

"If you can't sleep, don't count sheep. Talk to the Shepherd."

"No God—No Peace. Know God—Know Peace."

"God so loved the world that He did not send a committee."

"Fight Truth Decay—Read the Bible!"

"If you're headed in the wrong direction, God allows for U-turns."

"If you don't like the way you were born, try being born again."

"It is unlikely there'll be a reduction in the wages of sin."

"The best vitamin for a Christian is B1."

"Soul food served here."

"Beat the Christmas rush, come to church this Sunday."

"Don't give up. Moses was once a basket case!"

"What part of 'Thou shalt not' don't you understand?"

"To belittle is to be little."

"So live that no matter what happens, it wouldn't happen to a nicer person."

"After two thousand years, we are still under the same management."

"It sure is strange how little things can bug us! For instance, it's a lot easier to sit on a mountaintop than a tack."

THE FALL

A man named Jack was walking along a steep cliff one day when he accidentally got too close to the edge and fell. On the way down he grabbed a branch, which temporarily stopped his fall. He looked down and to his horror saw that the drop below him was more than a thousand feet, and he couldn't hang on to the branch forever.

So Jack began yelling for help, hoping that someone passing by would hear and lower a rope or do something.

"Help! Help! Is anyone up there? Help!" Jack yelled. No one heard him. He was about to give up when he heard a voice, "Jack, Jack. Can you hear me?"

"Yes, yes! I can hear you. I'm down here!"

"I can see you, Jack. Are you all right?"

"No! Yes! But, who are you, and where are you?"

"I am the Lord, Jack. I'm everywhere."

"The Lord? You mean GOD?"

"That's me."

"Oh, God, please help me! I promise that if You get me down from here, I'll really be a good person. I'll go back to church and serve you for the rest of my life."

"Easy on the promises, Jack. Now, here's what I want you to do. Listen carefully."

"I'll do anything, Lord. Just tell me."

"Okay. Let go of the branch."

"What?"

"I said, let go of the branch. Trust me. Let go."

There was a long silence.

Finally Jack yelled, "Help! Help! Help! Is there anyone else up there?"

PROVERBS FOR THE TWENTY-FIRST CENTURY

The children's Sunday school department was undertaking a study of the Book of Proverbs. To illustrate what proverbs are, Miss Daisy collected the first phrase of a bunch of traditional ones and asked the children to creatively complete them. Here are some results:

Better to be safe than. . .punch a
fifth-grader.
Strike while the. . .bug is close.
Don't bite the hand that. . .looks dirty.
The pen is mightier than the. . .pigs.
A penny saved. . .is not very much.
Children should be seen and not. . .
spanked or grounded.

Lesson in Forgiveness

"Forgive your enemies" was the topic of the reverend's sermon on this particular Sunday morning. At the close of his rather long message, he asked how many were willing to forgive their enemies. About half of his congregation raised their hands.

Not satisfied, he preached for another twenty minutes and repeated the question. This time a few more lifted their hands.

Still unsatisfied he lectured another fifteen minutes and repeated the question. Now, all raised their hands except one elderly lady on the back row. "Miz Jones, aren't you willing to forgive your enemies?" the pastor inquired.

"I don't have any" was her answer.

"Miz Jones, that's very unusual. How old are you?"

"Ninety-three."

"Miz Jones, please come down front and tell this congregation how a person can live ninety-three years and not have an enemy in the world."

The sweet little lady tottered down the aisle, very slowly turned around, and announced, "It's easy. I just outlived 'em all!"

BELL RINGER

Centuries before mega-churches built in the burbs and introduced awesome electric signage, churches attracted attention with cross-topped steeples. The taller the better. So, once upon a time, there was a village church with a steeple that could be seen for miles around. It was perfect, except for one thing—the bell wouldn't ring.

The church fathers invited people from all around to try their hands at remedying the problem—but to no avail.

One day a small fellow came to the church and announced to the pastor, "I can make the bell ring."

The pastor said, "Okay, try it."

So the little guy climbed up to the base of the belfry in the steeple, took three steps back, and then ran into the bell with his face. BONG! The bell rang, and he was hired on the spot.

One windy day, as the little man ran toward the bell, the wind moved it, causing the small bell ringer to fall out of the steeple and onto the ground below. As a crowd gathered, the pastor asked, "Does anyone know this fellow's name?" Just then a woman bent low to look at him and then replied, "I don't know his name, but his face sure rings a bell."

REASONS

Some go to church to take a walk;
Some go there to laugh and talk;
Some go there to meet a friend;
Some go there their time to spend;
Some go there to meet a lover;
Some go there a fault to cover;
Some go there for speculation;
Some go there for observation;
Some go there to doze and nod;
The wise go there to worship God.

A Lesson Learned

A young evangelist had just begun his first full-time job. He was unsettled one morning when he heard a church board member boasting how he used a radar detector to avoid getting ticketed for speeding. A moment later he was pleased to hear another member tell the man, "It's the man upstairs that you need to be worried about."

The young evangelist was just about to offer his appreciation for the second man's honesty when he added, "That guy in the helicopter will get you every time!"

Slightly Askew

According to Donna Miller, Adam and Eve were created from an apple tree. Noah's wife was called Joan of Ark. Noah built an ark, which the animal came onto in pears.

MARRIAGE EXAM

When the pastor of Bay Shore Community Church introduced his midweek study on marriage, he asked the younger Sunday school kids to answer a series of questions about the great institution.

Q: What is the proper age to marry?
A: "Eighty-four. Because at that age you don't have to work any more, and you can spend all your time loving each other."

Q: When is it okay to kiss someone?
A: "Never kiss in front of other people. It's a big embarrassing thing if anyone sees you. But if nobody sees you, I might be willing to try it with a handsome boy, but just for a few hours."

Q: Is it better to be single or married?
A: "It's better for girls to be single, but not for boys. Boys need somebody to clean up after them."

Q: How does love happen between two people?

A: "I think you're supposed to be shot with an arrow or something, but the rest isn't supposed to be so painful."

Q: What is falling in love like?

A: "Like an avalanche where you have to run for your life."

Q: Why do lovers hold hands?

A: "They want to make sure their rings don't fall off, because they paid good money for them."

Q: How does a person learn to kiss?

A: "You learn right on the spot, when the 'gooshy' feelings get the best of you."

Q: How do you make love endure?

A: "Don't forget your wife's name—that will mess up the love."

A: "Be a good kisser. It might make your wife forget that you never take the trash out."

A Test of Faith

I was listening to Christian radio and heard a lady call in. "Pastor, I was born blind, and I've been blind all my life. I don't mind so much being blind, but I have some well-meaning friends who tell me that if I had more faith I could be healed."

The radio pastor asked her, "Tell me, do you carry one of those white canes?"

"Yes, I do," she answered.

"Then the next time someone tells you that, hit him or her on the head with your cane and say, 'If you had more faith that wouldn't hurt.'"

Preaching Suggestion

All public speakers can learn from this true story. There are certain tribes in Africa that demand that when a man rises to speak, he must stand on one foot while delivering his speech. The minute the lifted foot touches the ground, the speech ends—or the speaker is forcibly silenced.

TOP SEVEN CHURCH OXYMORONS

Brief meeting
Pastor's day off
Early sign up
Clear calendar
Volunteer waiting list
Realistic budget
Concluding remarks

WORD ASSOCIATION

A lecturer from the denominational seminary was illustrating some point or other in an adult education class. "What is the opposite of 'joy'?"

" 'Sadness,' " answered the student.

The academic nodded approvingly and continued, "And the opposite of 'depression'?"

" 'Elation,' " another student volunteered.

Undeterred the lecturer persisted with her questioning, "And what about the opposite of 'woe'?"

Quick as a flash, an old-timer in the

class fired back, "I reckon that would be 'giddy up.' "

THE RITE OF BAPTISM

A Presbyterian minister was about to baptize a baby. Turning to the father, he inquired, "His name, please?"

"William Patrick Arthur Timothy John MacArthur," the father announced.

The minister turned to his assistant and said, "A little more water, please."

"I don't mind going to a church service in a drive-in theatre. But when they hold the baptisms in a car wash, that's going too far."

CHURCH COMMENTS

"The average man's idea of a good sermon is one that goes over his head and hits a neighbor."

"If all the people in church were laid end to end, they would be. . .more comfortable."

"He was said to be a great preacher—at the close of every sermon there was a great awakening."

"Be a peacemaker. . .always remember that it's hard to shake hands with a clenched fist."

A TEACHING

When Pastor Jackson over at Second Presbyterian got fed up with all the excuses folks give for not attending church, he offered his own list: "Ten Reasons Not to Wash."
1. I was forced to as a child.
2. People who wash are hypocrites—they think they are cleaner than everybody else.
3. There are so many different kinds of soap, I can't decide which is best.

4. I used to wash, but I got bored
    and stopped.
5. I wash only on special occasions,
    like Christmas and Easter.
6. None of my friends wash.
7. I'll start washing when I get older
    and dirtier.
8. I can't spare the time.
9. The bathroom is never warm
    enough in winter or cool enough
    in summer.
10. People who make soap are only after
    your money.

TRUE EVANGELISM

Ten little Christians standing in line. One
disliked the preacher, then there were nine.

Nine little Christians stayed up very
late. One overslept Sunday, then there
were eight.

Eight little Christians on their way to
heaven. One took the low road, and then
there were seven.

Seven little Christians chirping like chicks. One disliked the music, then there were six.

Six little Christians seemed very much alive, but one lost his interest, then there were five.

Five little Christians pulling for heaven's shore, but one stopped to rest, then there were four.

Four little Christians, each busy as a bee. One got his feelings hurt, then there were three.

Three little Christians knew not what to do. One joined the sporty crowd, then there were two.

Two little Christians, our rhyme is nearly done, differed with each other, then there was one.

One little Christian can't do much 'tis true, brought his friend to Bible study, then there were two.

Two earnest Christians, each won one more. That doubled the number, then there were four.

Four sincere Christians worked early

and late. Each won another, then there were eight.

Eight splendid Christians if they doubled as before, in just seven Sundays, we'd have 1,024.

A Jingle

In this little jingle, there is a lesson true, you belong either to the building or to the wrecking crew.

Target Audience

Did you hear about the just-out-of-seminary-pastor who practiced what he preached? He didn't stand at the door and shake hands with the worshipers after the service. He went out to the curb and shook hands with the red-faced parents waiting for their children to come out of Sunday school.

THE SWEET BY 'N BY

The number one topic in the category of church and religious jokes is old age, coupled with St. Peter and the pearly gates. (A popular cartoon has the heavenly gatekeeper sitting at his computer and telling the poor soul standing before him, "Sorry, bub. You're not in the database.")

As the title implies, this chapter looks to "that beautiful shore." Makes one wonder why death and the future life are so funny to the average joke teller. Maybe it's the comedian's personal wrestle with the spiritual. ("My greatest fear is that I'll be standing behind Mother Teresa in the Final Judgment line, and I'll hear God tell her, 'You know, you should have done more.' ")

Someone else has suggested, "You should die laughing."

NEAR DEATH EXPERIENCE

Bertha Jones was a middle-aged woman who had a heart attack and was taken to the hospital. While on the operating table she had a near death experience. During that experience she saw God and asked if this was the end of the road for her. God said no and explained that she had another thirty years to live.

Upon her recovery she figured if she had thirty to forty more years, she might as well stay in the hospital and have a face-lift, liposuction, tummy tuck, hair transplant and coloring, and a nose job.

After her hospital stay, she walked out of the front door and was killed by a delivery truck. When she arrived in front of God, she asked, "I thought you said I had another thirty to forty years left?"

God replied, "Sorry, Bertha, I didn't recognize you."

A Limerick

There once was a pious young priest
Who lived almost wholly on yeast,
He said, "For it's plain
We must all rise again,
And I wanted to get started, at least."

Vote!

A parishioner had dozed off to sleep during the morning service.

"Will all who want to go to heaven stand up now."

All stood, except the sleeping parishioner.

After they sat, the pastor continued, "Well, will all who want to go to the other place please stand?" Somebody suddenly dropped a hymnal, and the sleeping man jumped to his feet and stood sheepishly facing the preacher.

The sleeper mumbled confused. "Well, preacher, I don't know what we're voting for, but it looks like you and I are the only ones for it."

READER

Mattie George was a first-class church lady and constant Bible reader. When asked why she did not try a more varied reading, Mattie replied, "I can't. I'm cramming for my finals."

GRACE

When Brother Martin died and went to heaven, he was met at the front gate by St. Peter, who let him know that he needed one hundred points to make it in the pearly gates. "You tell me all the good things you've done, and I'll give you points according to your deeds. When you reach one hundred, I'll swing open the gates."

"Okay," Ted reported, "I was head usher at First Baptist for fifty years."

"That's wonderful," says St. Peter, "that's worth two points."

"I was married to the same woman for almost sixty-five years and never cheated on her."

"Remarkable," Peter declared, "here are three more points."

"Only three?" Ted frowned. "How about this? I started a soup kitchen in the inner city and worked in a homeless shelter."

"Terrific, and here are two more points."

Ted's eyes opened wide, and he yelled, "Two points! At this rate the only way I'll get into heaven is by the grace of God!"

"Come on in!"

TIME'S A WASTIN'

A minister waited in line to have his car filled with gas before a long holiday weekend. The attendant worked quickly, but there were many cars in front and in back of him. Finally the attendant motioned him toward a vacant pump. "Reverend," said the young man, "sorry about the delay. It seems as if everyone waits until the last minute to get ready for a long trip."

The minister chuckled, "I know

exactly what you mean. It's the same in my business."

THREE-TIMER

Old Andy Kline passed on, and at the end of his church funeral, someone remarked, "As I recall, old Andy attended church only three times during his entire life—when he was hatched, when he was matched, and now, when dispatched!"

CARTOON CUTLINE

A sign painter is quizzing a robed prophet of doom. He asks, "You want that sign to read 'The world ends tomorrow'. . .when do you have to have it?"

PITCHER UP!

Hank and Frank were baseball buddies. They were the biggest fans in the whole U.S. Both were stars on the Faith Church team, Third Baptist team, and coached the little boys T-Ball for elementary school teams.

The guys made an agreement between them that whoever died first would try to come back and report on whether or not there was baseball in heaven.

Hank died first, and as he promised, came to Frank as in a dream. "Frank, Frank," Hank whispered into his buddy's ear, "I've got good news and I've got bad news. The good news is that there is baseball in heaven."

"And the bad news?" Frank asked.

"You're pitching tomorrow night!"

LAST WORDS

There were three men standing at the gates of heaven with St. Peter. "Tell me, what would you like to hear your relatives or friends say at your funeral?" the Saint asked.

The first man answered, "Because I'm

a renowned physician, I'd love to hear someone say how I'd been instrumental in saving someone's life."

The second man reported that he was a family man and a schoolteacher and that it would be wonderful if someone said that he had been a wonderful father and husband and that he had made a difference in some young person's life.

The third man before St. Peter said, "Wow, you guys, those are really great sentiments, but I guess if I had my choice, I would hear someone say, 'Look! He's moving!'"

DEAR PASTOR. . .

"I hope to go to heaven someday, but make it later than sooner."

Ellen, age nine

"I would like to go to heaven someday because I know my brother won't be there."

Stephen, age eight

OLD AGE

At the church's Golden-Agers banquet, the following was shared by Sister Bertha. She began her piece by saying, "You can tell you're getting older and heading toward the sweet by 'n by when. . ."

You sit in a rocking chair and can't get it going.

You burn the midnight oil after 8:00 P.M.

You look forward to a dull evening.

Your knees buckle and your belt won't.

Your little black book contains only names ending in M.D.

Your back goes out more than you do.

You decide to procrastinate and never get around to it.

Dialing long distance wears you out.

You walk with your head held high, trying to get used to your bifocals.

You sink your teeth into a steak, and they stay there.

HEREAFTER

The preacher told me the other day I should be thinking about the Hereafter.

I told him, "I do, all the time. No matter where I am—in the parlor, upstairs, in the kitchen, or in the basement. I'm always asking myself, 'Now, what am I here after?'"

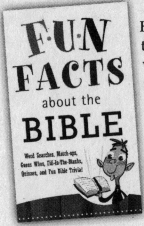